The Calotype Process

SUTTON'S CALOTYPE PROCESS.

Unwashed Iodized Paper.

Washed Iodized Paper.

PHOTOGRAPHIC INSTITUTION, 168 NEW BOND STREET.

THE CALOTYPE PROCESS.

A Hand Book

TO

PHOTOGRAPHY ON PAPER.

BY

THOMAS SUTTON, B.A.

CAIUS COLL. CAMBRIDGE.

LONDON:
PUBLISHED BY JOSEPH CUNDALL,
AT THE PHOTOGRAPHIC INSTITUTION, 168 NEW BOND STREET;
AND BY SAMPSON LOW AND SON, 47 LUDGATE HILL.
1855.

LONDON:
Printed by G. BARCLAY, Castle St. Leicester Sq.

CONTENTS.

	PAGE
PREFACE	v
INTRODUCTION	1
The Positive	—
Printing	2
The Negative	—
THE NEGATIVE PROCESS	7
Chemicals	8
Apparatus, &c.	9
First Operation; to Iodize the Paper	11
1. By Floatation	12
2. By Brushing	15
To wash the Iodized Papers	16
Second Operation; to Sensitize the Paper	19
Aceto-Nitrate of Silver	21
Saturated Solution of Gallic Acid	22
The Sensitive Solution	—
To apply it	23
Third Operation; to Expose in the Camera	25
The Time of Exposure	29
Fourth Operation; to Develope the Image	34
The Developing Solution	35
To apply it, &c.	36

CONTENTS.

	PAGE
Fifth Operation ; to Fix the Picture	38
Sixth Operation ; to Wax, &c.	40
The Waxing-apparatus	41
To Wax large Pictures	42
CAUSES OF FAILURE	44
THE PRINTING PROCESS	49
Chemicals	50
Printing-Room	51
Apparatus	—
First Operation ; to Salt the Papers	52
Salted Papers	—
Albumenized and Salted	53
Second Operation ; to Sensitize the Papers	55
Sensitive Solution	—
Third Operation ; to Expose in the Pressure-Frame	57
The Pressure-Frame	58
The Exposure	—
Fourth Operation ; to Fix and Tone the Print	62
Fixing and Toning-Baths	—
Fifth Operation ; to Trim and Mount	66
THE FRENCH VIOLET TINTS	67
To Mount Positives behind a Glass	72
NOTES	77

PREFACE.

THE following pages have been written under the strong conviction, that in the present state of photographic literature, it is utterly useless to multiply works of this class, unless the author resolves, in the first place, to describe *his own particular process*, and that only; and, secondly, to deal with that so *faithfully* and *minutely*, as that he may be followed by his reader with nearly the same degree of certainty as though he had been seen at work at it himself. For the difference between success and failure seems now to consist in attention *to minutiæ* and to the *niceties of manipulation*, rather than in any *diversity of the materials* employed, or any *striking novelty* in the mode of using them.

I am at present but little known to the photographic world, but the name of my publisher, who has himself witnessed the process in all its stages, will, I trust, be a sufficient guarantee for the truth of the following assertions in its favour.

In the first place, I maintain, that if the manipulator will carefully attend to the directions hereafter given, he will find the process, if not *absolutely* unfailing, at all events *very nearly* a CERTAIN one. And this certainty arises from the fact, that the time of exposure in the camera is not in *this*, that critical feature of the operation that it is in the *collodion* and the *waxed-paper* processes; for here, provided the picture be but exposed *long enough* for the complete rendering of the work in the shadows, it may then be exposed to a *considerable extent beyond* this point, without necessarily reddening the blacks, or embrowning the whites; since the mode of development which follows can be adapted to the aspect of the picture when taken from the slide, and in this way, good blacks and clean whites may always be obtained.

Secondly, that it is a process peculiarly adapted to THE TOURIST, since it requires but little apparatus, and involves the least possible amount of disorder or untidiness at inns; for I assume the bed-room of a hotel or lodging-house to be the scene of the greater part of the processes, and I adapt my description of them to meet the inconveniences of this sort of manipulating room.

And, finally, that by this process, and, as I think, BY THIS EXCLUSIVELY, an enlarged field of action becomes open to the successful amateur, in the ready means which it affords for the production of GRAND AND IMPOSING PICTURES, such as may represent faithfully, and artistically, the finest objects and scenery in the world, and of *such a size* and quality as may render them worthy to become fellow-occupants, on the walls of our rooms and galleries, with the best engravings and paintings. For the manipulation of these large works is exactly similar to that of the small ones, and involves no increased risk of failure whatever.

Such are the merits of this process. It is a dry one upon paper not previously waxed, and it resembles in all its main points the original "Calotype" process, modified by certain slight, and perhaps apparently trivial, differences of manipulation; but, as I have said before, it is *exactly through attention to these little matters* that success and certainty are to be obtained, and I therefore desire to lay great stress upon them.

I have throughout assumed no previous photographic knowledge whatever on the part of the reader, and when the *theory* of any operation under discussion can be satisfactorily made out, I have given it to the best of my ability.

Not to interrupt too frequently the thread of the description, I have adopted the plan of giving references to Notes at the end.

Should this process, as I have described it, appear to the reader, *at first sight*, to be somewhat tedious and difficult, I must beg of him to bear in mind, that the attempt to convey an accurate idea, by *words*, of even the simplest manual operation, will be found by no means a brief or an easy one; what then is likely to be the case with such a subject as the present? I can assure him, honestly, that the process is, in fact, when once it shall have become familiar, *an exceedingly easy and simple one.*

In describing the Printing process, I have given, in addition to the usual formula for albumenised paper, the method of obtaining the RICH DARK VIOLET TONES of the French photographers, without the aid of old hyposulphite; and also, a new and very effective mode of MOUNTING positives, which secures to them all the transparency which they may possess when in water.

In conclusion, I may add, that I have taken the *utmost pains* to avoid the omission of anything which might conduce, in other hands, to the enjoyment of the same certainty that, I am happy to say, I have of late experienced myself. In return, it will be but fair in others to withhold their condemnation till they have made an *honest* trial of the process, as it stands recorded here, in every particular.

THOMAS SUTTON.

St. Brelade's Bay, Jersey,
March 1855.

INTRODUCTION.

THE finished photograph on paper, which is usually mounted on cardboard, and thus offered for inspection and criticism, is called, in common parlance amongst photographers, a "Positive print," or simply a "Print." It should represent objects faithfully, and without distortion, in the same manner as an engraving or a drawing,—that is to say, the lights and shadows should be true to nature, the objects in their proper places (and not reversed), and the conditions imposed by the laws of plane perspective rigorously fulfilled. The Positive.

Our aim, therefore, in all our operations, is to obtain finally this Positive photograph, or Print.

The Positive, however, is not, in the paper process, obtained *at once* (as in the daguerreotype) from the objects as they stand, but through the medium of another photograph of the same objects previously obtained, and called the "Negative;" and by a process termed "Printing," which may either be executed at home by the amateur himself, or in printing establishments devoted to that particular branch of the art.

Printing.

The negative, therefore, must *first* be taken, and that by means of apparatus conveyed to the spot. In it the lights and shadows are all *reversed*,—the sky and high *lights* of the objects being rendered by *blacks*, the deepest *shadows* by *lights*, and the intermediate shades by the corresponding intermediate gradations of tint. The position, also, of the objects, as regards right and left, is reversed; and to judge of the merits of a negative it becomes necessary to view it by transparency, and with its back to the eye.

The negative

viewed by transparency.

There are, therefore, in photography on paper, two distinct operations,—

1. The production of the *Negative*.
2. The printing of the *Positive*.

Both operations are equally important; for although with a feeble and imperfect negative it is impossible to produce a rich and good positive, yet even *with* a good negative it is perfectly possible to produce a very inferior and bad positive. Both must be equally well done to ensure the reward for which the photographer has to encounter no inconsiderable amount of trouble and difficulty.

INTRODUCTION. 3

An unlimited number of prints may be taken from one single negative, and in this power of reproducing positives *ad infinitum* a great advantage is gained over the daguerreotype process. Hence it becomes evident that no amount of pains or trouble should be spared in the production of a good negative, —a work not to be undertaken hastily, or carelessly, or by the dozen, but, on the contrary, one requiring considerable thought and study, as regards the artistic composition of the picture, the proper effect of light and shade, &c. &c. So that, to attempt to avoid any part of the necessary *mechanical* trouble, and thereby to introduce the risk of failure, or the certainty of some inferiority in the result, would be unworthy and puerile in the extreme. Under this conviction, and at the risk of being thought sometimes unnecessarily prolix, I shall not hesitate to describe *most minutely* all matters connected with this important part of the subject, which I consider to be worthy of attention as conducing to a satisfactory result, and this quite irrespective of any additional trouble in the manipulation.

To proceed, then, in the proper order of work, we commence with the Negative Process.

No pains should be spared in the production of the negative.

THE NEGATIVE PROCESS.

THE NEGATIVE PROCESS.

This process involves six distinct operations, viz.—

1. To *iodize* the paper.
2. To render it *sensitive* to light.
3. To *expose* it in the camera.
4. To *develope* the picture.
5. To *fix* the picture.
6. To *wax*, trim, &c., the finished picture.

The first of these processes may be done at home, and at leisure. The iodized papers may be preserved for an indefinite time, and a stock of them should always be kept on hand. The second, third, fourth and fifth processes are performed " *en route;*" and the sixth at home, at any convenient opportunity.

CHEMICALS.

The chemicals required in the negative process are the following:

Nitrate of silver, crystallized or fused (Note 1).
Iodide of potassium.
Gallic acid.
Glacial acetic acid (Note 2).
Hyposulphite of soda.
Distilled water.

These chemicals may be obtained of sufficient purity, from all respectable photographic chemists.

The first three should be kept in *wide*-mouthed stoppered bottles, the acetic acid in a *small*-mouthed stoppered bottle, the hyposulphite in a wide-mouthed bottle with a cork, or in a large earthen jar with a lid, and the distilled water in a half-gallon bottle with a glass stopper.

One ounce of nitrate of silver, one ounce of iodide of potassium, one ounce of acetic acid, half-an-ounce of gallic acid, and one pound of hyposulphite of soda, will suffice for several experiments.

The chemicals should be kept in a dry and cool place.

APPARATUS, &c.

The apparatus, and other articles required in the negative process, are—

1.—TO ACCOMPANY THE TOURIST.

The lens (Note 3).
The camera (Note 4).
The stand (Note 5).
The focussing screen (Note 6).
The dark slide (Note 7).
A small spirit-level.
Two dark Macintosh cloths, of different sizes.
A box of scales and weights.
Glass developing-slab.
Deal board.
Portfolio, containing blotting-paper, &c. &c.
Two zinc dishes; one with a thin removable gutta-percha lining.
Magnifying glass (Note 19).
Wooden paper-clips (Note 11).
Glass tubes (Note 12).
Cotton wool, *chemically clean*.

All these articles, and certain chemicals besides, will be required "*en route.*" It may seem to be, at the *first glance*, a somewhat lengthy catalogue; but, in fact, they will all be found to pack together very easily, and to form by no means a cumbrous parcel.

2.—At Home.

Several dishes, made either of earthenware, or of zinc with gutta-percha linings; in which to wash iodized papers.

A zinc apparatus for waxing negatives.

An iodizing brush, of camel's hair, bound with silver wire.

A graduated bottle for double iodide.

A funnel and stand for the same.

A one-ounce glass measure.

A porcelain capsule and stand.

A spirit-lamp.

A glass mortar and pestle.

The three last-mentioned articles will only be required, when it is thought advisable to fuse the nitrate of silver.

FIRST OPERATION.

To Iodize the Paper.

The whole of this process may be performed by daylight; and it consists in the impregnation of the paper with the yellow iodide of silver.

The following is a preliminary sketch of it:—

The yellow iodide of silver is a powder, insoluble in water, and in order to apply it to the paper it is first dissolved in a strong solution of iodide of potassium, forming what is called "double iodide." This solution is then applied in the usual way, either by brushing, or floatation upon a bath; and the paper hung up to dry. When dry, it is placed in water for some hours, and the iodide of potassium dissolved out, leaving the yellow iodide of silver upon the surface, and in the pores of the paper, which is then dried again, and preserved in a portfolio until required for use. *[Sketch of the iodizing process.]*

Such is a brief sketch of the iodizing process, and the *rationale* of it. The mode of obtaining the

12   THE NEGATIVE PROCESS.

double iodide is given at considerable length in Note 8; and I proceed now to describe more minutely the two different modes of applying it to the paper.

1.—By Floatation.

<small>Floating a good plan for wholesale work.</small>

This is an excellent plan when papers are to be iodized *for commerce,* and in large quantities; but it will be found a somewhat costly one for the amateur, since a considerable quantity of expensive material is required in the first instance to fill a bath of large size.

Proceed thus,

<small>Size of sheets.</small>

First, cut the requisite quantity of PAPER (see Note 9) to the proper size of each sheet, and make a pencil-mark upon the *back* of each sheet at one extreme corner. The sheets should be equal in width, and half an inch longer than the glass of the dark slide.

<small>The bath.</small>

Place a shallow bath of plate-glass (Note 10), (*which should be set apart for this purpose exclusively*), upon a table, in a *perfectly horizontal* position between yourself and the window; and about breast-high, if possible; and having seen previously, that it is not only clean, but *dry* (for if at all *wet*, it would render the solution turbid), pour the filtered double

TO IODIZE THE PAPER.

iodide into it, to a depth of about three-sixteenths of an inch, and clear the surface from all air-bubbles. Then float the face of the paper upon it in the following manner:—Fold back a quarter of an inch at the narrow end of the paper, in such a manner that it shall not be wetted by the solution, then take an end corner in each hand, and suspend the paper vertically, with its lower edge upon the fluid, at a distance of an inch or two from that end of the bath which is nearest to you. Then gradually depress it upon the fluid, pushing the edge first in contact along the surface, until it reaches the farther end of the bath; then allow the upper edge of the paper to drop gently on to the liquid. *[To float the paper on the bath.]*

In performing this operation, *take great care that the back of the paper be not wetted;* also, that no dry spots occur, untouched by the solution.

Allow the papers to remain upon the bath for two or three minutes, then drain them into it for an instant, and hang them up to dry, attaching a narrow strip of blotting-paper to the lower corner, to facilitate the draining off of the superfluous fluid. They may be suspended, either by means of pins, or needles with sealing-wax heads, or better still, by wooden clips (Note 11). *When pins are used, it is absolutely necessary that the chemicals should not touch them,* as this would occasion a stain, which might extend for some distance down the paper. *[Time on the bath.]* *[To suspend them.]*

To guard against this danger, pass the pins through the *dry* band which was folded back. Small papers may be suspended by one corner, but large ones will require to be suspended by the whole of the dry band, with three or four pins or clips.

<small>To remove the paper from the bath.</small>

The neatest way of removing a paper from the bath is to raise one corner by means of a strip of glass held in the left hand, and to seize that corner by a clip held in the other. When three or four clips are necessary, proceed thus:—Attach them all at the proper points before removing the paper, and allow them to hang over the edge of the bath; then pass a rod of wood like a yard-measure through all the loops, and raise the paper by it, holding it in the middle. In this way the assistance of a second person will be unnecessary. The rod with the paper hanging from it may be supported upon two round hooks screwed into the under side of a bar of wood. It is obvious that for this manœuvre the loops and clips should be all of the same length.

<small>Suspension of large papers by clips.</small>

The bath must be replenished as occasion may require; and never allowed to get too low.

When dry, the papers will have a reddish tint. They may be put away in a portfolio, until it is found convenient to wash them.

2.—BY BRUSHING.

This is the plan which I recommend to the amateur. It answers *perfectly well* when managed with a little dexterity, which is soon acquired by practice. The brush should be a large round one, of camel's hair, *bound with silver wire,* and set apart for this purpose *exclusively*.

[Marginal note: Brushing the best plan for amateurs. The Brush]

Take a soft pine board, a little larger than the paper,—upon this lay a sheet of clean white blotting-paper, and upon that the sheet of negative paper to be iodized, face upwards, having previously made a pencil-mark upon *its back*, at one corner. Pin it to the board by the two upper corners. Then pour the double iodide into a clean and *dry* wine-glass, and let the brush be perfectly *dry* when first dipped in, or it will render the solution turbid. Hold the board in the left hand, between yourself and the light, and inclining it gently, apply the solution with a *full* brush, copiously and fearlessly,—first, longitudinally all over, and then transversely all over, *precisely in the same manner as if laying on a broad sky wash in water-colours, and always keeping a flowing edge*. Take care not to let the solution run beyond the edge of the paper, or touch the pins. This done, hang up to dry as before, either by pins or clips.

[Marginal note: To apply the solution with the brush.]

THE NEGATIVE PROCESS.

The iodizing being now effected either by floatation or brushing, and the papers being dry, the next operation will be

To Wash the Iodized Papers,

in order to remove THE WHOLE of the iodide of potassium, and to deposit the yellow iodide of silver upon, and in the pores of the paper. *And it is of the utmost importance that the* WHOLE *of this iodide of potassium should be removed.* It has merely served as *the vehicle* for the conveyance of the iodide of silver to the paper; and if allowed to remain, it would instantly decompose the sensitive solution to be afterwards applied, and would render that part of the paper insensible to light, leaving there a *white blotch,* which would be ruinous to the picture. The importance, therefore, of the *thorough washing,* which I am about to describe, cannot be too much insisted on; as, if imperfectly and carelessly done, success in the after stages of the work will be *impossible.*

<small>The whole of the iodide of potassium must be removed by washing.</small>

<small>The dishes.</small> The iodized papers, when of small size, may be washed in earthenware dishes, kept for this purpose, and never used for any other; or, when of large size, in dishes made of zinc, about two inches deep, and furnished with a removable *thin* gutta-percha

TO IODIZE THE PAPER. 17

lining. The sides of these dishes, of whatever material, should be upright (or very *slightly* inclined outwards), and should by no means have lips at the corners, which, I think, a great mistake; as, on agitating the contents of the dish, the fluid is very likely to run over at one or all of these lips, unless *excessive* care be taken to prevent it. The dishes should be sufficiently large to allow the paper to be entirely and constantly submerged. Dishes without lips are to be preferred.

Fill the dish completely with common water, and first, place the paper face downwards upon it. Let it remain a minute; then remove it, and place it face upwards. Now, with a long feather, or with the iodizing brush previously washed, remove most carefully all air-bubbles from the face, and wet it in every part. Then turn it over, and do the same to the back, leaving it back upwards in the water. In a few minutes the back will be seen, in all probability, *covered with minute air-bubbles; brush these off* as before; and change the water in about half - an - hour, removing the air - bubbles a second time, if necessary, *as these would occasion small white spots in the negative.* Allow the paper to remain face downwards in the water for twenty-four hours; agitate it occasionally, and change the water for the last time just before taking the paper out. Dry it by suspension, as described before; and To wash the iodized papers. Remove small air-bubbles. Papers to remain in water for 24 hours.

c

18   THE NEGATIVE PROCESS.

when dry, put it away carefully in a separate portfolio, which keep always in a dry place.

Changes of colour.

The following are the changes of colour which the paper undergoes. Before washing, it is of a *reddish* tint; on immersion, it speedily changes to a *blue* or *grey*; and, in the course of an hour or so, to a *yellow*, which is its final colour.

Only one paper in one dish.

The washing should not be attempted in very cold, frosty weather; *nor should more than one paper be placed in a dish at a time.* The number of papers which may be washed in one day, will therefore depend upon the number of dishes devoted to this purpose.

Long soaking gives better definition.

Better definition is, I find, obtainable upon papers which have been in water for twenty-four hours than upon those which have only been immersed for ten or twelve; very possibly in consequence of the iodide of potassium having been more thoroughly and completely removed, in the former case, from the *minutest pores* of the paper.

Iodized papers will keep indefinitely.

As I have before remarked, the yellow iodized papers may be preserved indefinitely; and now assuming the first process, viz. that of iodizing, to have been thoroughly understood, and accomplished at home, and a good stock of papers to have been procured, I shall imagine the scene of operations transferred to the room of an inn or a house in the neighbourhood of the views to be taken, and shall proceed to the second operation, viz., to render the iodized papers sensitive to light.

SECOND OPERATION.

To render the Iodized Paper sensitive to Light.

The process of iodizing has been performed in ordinary daylight, the iodized papers not being sensitive to light; but in the sensitizing of them, it is obvious that we must manipulate in a light which is *not* " actinic" (or, in other words, which is *not* capable of producing a chemical change on a sensitive surface). A *yellow* light has, happily for our present purpose, this advantage (otherwise the unfortunate photographer would be condemned to work in *total darkness*, guided only by the sense of touch); and we may, therefore, avail ourselves of the yellow

<small>A yellow light necessary for sensitizing.</small>

Yellow calico screen to the window. light of a candle; or of daylight, admitted *in moderation*, through a double or triple thickness of yellow calico, placed in the window. This being the case, *any* room may be quickly rendered available for photographic purposes.

Better to sensitize on the day of taking the view. Sensitive papers generally retain their colour and good qualities for twenty-four hours, and sometimes even for several days. The sensitizing for the following day *may*, therefore, be effected over night, and by the light of a candle; but it is safer to defer it until the morning of the day on which the views are to be taken, as we are then *more certain of the weather;* and in this case, recourse must be had to the screen of yellow calico before the window.

To darken the room. Choose, therefore, if possible, a room with *only one* window. Pin before it (*inside* the room) a large dark macintosh cloth, in such a way as to leave about four square feet uncovered, and in front of the opening, pin a double or triple thickness of yellow *Drawing-pins.* calico. Drawing-pins, with flat brass heads, are better for this purpose than common pins, as they are much stronger, and may be carried in a flat piece of cork.

The dark cloth. The dark cloth should be composed of two layers of stuff, with india-rubber cement between them; and it will also be found useful for other purposes described hereafter.

Should the window be *small,* the yellow calico will suffice without the cloth.

The room being now darkened, the door should be secured against any sudden intrusion, and the sensitizing of the paper proceeded with.

All the chemicals which I have detailed as necessary to the negative process must accompany the tourist, with the exception of the iodide of potassium. In addition to these, there should be a one-ounce stoppered bottle in a wooden case, containing a solution called " aceto-nitrate of silver;" a pint stoppered bottle, containing " a saturated solution of gallic acid in distilled water;" and a bottle of strong solution of gum arabic, with a small brush to apply it with. The chemicals required "en route."

To make Aceto-Nitrate of Silver.

First scratch two marks upon the bottle which is to contain it; one at the level of six-and-a-half drachms of fluid, the other at the level of one ounce. Fill the bottle *accurately* to the lower mark with distilled water, and add 50 grains of nitrate of silver; when dissolved, add glacial acetic acid until the mixture rises to the level of the upper mark; then shake well together. This solution is called aceto-nitrate of silver, and should be kept in darkness. Aceto-nitrate of silver should be kept in the dark.

THE NEGATIVE PROCESS.

To make a Saturated Solution of Gallic Acid.

To one pint (or twenty ounces) of distilled water add one quarter of an ounce of gallic acid. Let the bottle, containing this solution, stand for half-an-hour in a jug of hot water; nearly the whole of the acid will then be dissolved. *On the following day* filter it, and it is ready for use. In the course of some few days the solution will become discoloured; and in this state it is better not to employ it, as it would certainly communicate a brown tinge to the paper, which is objectionable, although not absolutely fatal to the picture. A smaller quantity of gallic acid may be mixed, if preferred.

<small>Use a jug of hot water.</small>

The Sensitive Solution.

Into a *scrupulously clean* wine-glass (Note 14), previously rinsed with distilled water, put

<small>Gallo-nitrate of silver.</small>

1 ounce . . Distilled water
20 drops . . Aceto-nitrate of silver
20 drops . . Saturated solution of gallic acid

This is the *sensitive solution*; and it is called *weak* " gallo-nitrate of silver." (Note 13.)

<small>To count the drops.</small>

In order to count the drops easily, and at the same time to filter them, make two little paper fun-

TO SENSITIZE THE PAPER.

nels (one for each solution) with pieces of thin white blotting paper, two inches square, and pour half a thimble-full of the solution to be measured into each.

The gallo-nitrate is an exceedingly *unstable* compound, and very ready to decompose and turn brown. It must, therefore, be *used promptly,* and the surplus immediately *thrown away.* It should also never be exposed to a ray of white light; *and the glass which has once contained it should not be employed again for the same purpose, until it has undergone the thorough washing described in* Note 14. Gallo-nitrate very unstable. Glass should be well washed.

To Apply the Sensitive Solution.

Place a sheet of *clean white* blotting-paper upon a deal board, and upon this the iodized paper face upwards. Pin down the two upper corners, and apply the solution VERY COPIOUSLY with a Buckle's brush (Note 12), first longitudinally, and then transversely, precisely in the manner described for the double iodide. Then raise the paper dexterously by one corner, and holding it over a basin, allow the superfluous liquid to run off;—this done, replace it on the board, and blot off the remaining moisture from the surface with two or three sheets of *clean* blotting-paper; not rubbing *too hard,* but passing See page 13. Blot off the surface moisture.

the hand *rapidly* and *gently* over the surface, as long as any wet or shining patches appear.

The next operation is to attach the sensitive paper to the glass of the dark slide, which is a very simple matter, occupying only a minute or two, and is thus performed:—

<small>To attach the sensitive paper to the glass.</small> With a small camel's-hair brush apply a thin and narrow edging of strong gum arabic all round the glass plate, and then lay the paper with its *back* upon it, pressing down the edges with the thumb, to make them adhere firmly. Then trim the overlap of the edges with a pair of scissors, and place the glass in the slide, with the sensitive paper next to the front shutter. Shut it up securely, and let it lie in a *horizontal* position, and *face upwards*, until ready to be packed and conveyed to its destination.

<small>Advantages of this plan.</small> The paper will dry in a few minutes, and then lie as flat as the glass itself; and when exposed in the camera, nothing will intervene between it and the lens, either to disturb the focus, or absorb the light; but I have discussed the advantages of this method so fully in Note 7, that it is unnecessary to recapitulate them here.

All is now ready for the third operation.

THIRD OPERATION.

The Exposure in the Camera.

The point of view having been selected (if possible, on some previous day), *and the proper hour for taking the picture ascertained*, the following articles must be conveyed to the spot:—

    The folding portion of the camera.
    The front of the camera.
    The ground-glass screen.
    The dark slides.
    The lens.
    The stand.

The first three may form one parcel; they should be wrapped up (the glass screen between the other two) in the *large* macintosh cloth, and secured by leather straps with buckles. *[Mode of packing the apparatus.]*

The dark slides should form another parcel; and should be wrapped up in the *small* macintosh cloth, and secured by straps with buckles.

The lens should be carried in a leather case.

The stand should form another independent article.

Careful selection of the point of view.

On arriving at the intended locality, do not unadvisedly adopt the first spot that offers itself, but carefully reconnoitre the whole vicinity, and choose that point of view which seems to give the most artistic picture. It is obvious that, in some cases, a single yard to the right or left may make or mar the whole work. I invariably adopt the plan, now, of taking duplicates of the view;—not from the *same* point, but from *different* points, a few feet apart, and on the same level. When both pictures turn out well, *they are adapted to the stereoscope*, which is a great advantage. (Note 15.)

Duplicate views for the stereoscope.

The camera should not be placed nearer to any object that it is intended to include than double its height, or breadth.

The picture a matter of much study and taste.

The selection of the point of view, and of the picture to be taken, must necessarily be so much a *matter of taste,* that it is impossible to lay down any rules upon this subject. The amateur will at first, no doubt, commit many blunders; and will find a long *"pratique"* necessary, before his eye and taste shall have become tutored to the requirements of this particular branch of art. He should lose no opportunity of visiting galleries of photographs, and of comparing closely his own efforts with those of others. In particular, the general effects of opposing masses of light and shadow, and of gradations of distance, should be carefully studied. Also the *weak*

Galleries visited and comparisons made.

EXPOSURE IN THE CAMERA.

points of photography, — such as the monotony of the skies, and the absence of life-like figures, and of colour, should be carefully borne in mind; no less than its *strong* ones, — such as its marvellous truthfulness and minute detail, artistic rendering of foregrounds, rock, foliage, &c. And he will doubtless find, after a long and cultivated experience, that not merely grand ruins, or mountain-passes, or fantastic oddities, truthfully delineated, make good photographs; but that nature has been bountiful to nearly every locality, and that many a charming "little bit" of rustic simplicity, which he may have passed by in his novitiate as too common-place, may really have been well worthy of his attention. *[The weak and strong points of photography should be borne in mind.]*

When the view is decided upon, plant the stand *firmly* upon the ground — for if it should move *but a single hair's breadth*, whilst the camera is at work, the picture will be spoiled. Never trust to grass, or soft earth, or a damp sandy beach; but thrust the legs firmly into *solid ground*, or find *three flat stones* to place underneath them. *[To plant the stand.]*

Having firmly planted the stand, put the camera together and mount it in its place; then, by means of a small pocket spirit-level, make the top truly horizontal. Next wipe the lens, if necessary, with a cambric handkerchief (not a silk one), and screw it *[To fix the camera, &c.]*

on; then put the ground glass into its place, and throwing the large macintosh cloth over the camera and your own head and shoulders, proceed to adjust the instrument and to focus the view as accurately as possible, with the help, if necessary, of a small magnifying glass. Should there be too much foreground, *raise* the slide which carries the lens to a suitable height; or if too much sky, *depress* it. *You should never elevate or depress the camera itself*, if it be possible to avoid doing so;—since, in the former case, all the vertical lines of the picture would tend to a vanishing point *above,* and in the latter to one *beneath* it, instead of being exactly perpendicular; which gives to buildings a very unsightly appearance. Now, remove the ground-glass screen; give the thumbscrew, which secures the camera to the stand, an extra turn, to ensure perfect steadiness; place the cap on the lens; and, having satisfied yourself that no light can enter the instrument through any crevices, put the dark slide into its place; raise the shutter; and throw the large macintosh cloth over the top of the camera, fastening it underneath by means of the straps, if there should be much wind.

All is now ready for the exposure.

Remove the cap from the lens, and note the exact time by your watch.

Margin notes: See note 19. | Camera should always be level. | See that no light can enter.

The Time of Exposure.

Photography has not yet arrived at perfection; and we are unable, at present, to take views *instantaneously* with certainty; *some* definite time of exposure is necessary, to enable the light sufficiently to impress the sensitive surface. In the daguerreotype, the collodion, and the waxed-paper processes, this time of exposure is a matter of *great nicety;* for a picture taken by any of these methods, when *under*-exposed, is defective in the details of the shadows; and when *over*-exposed, is solarized, or enfeebled and reddened. But in the process which I am advocating here, *greater latitude is allowable, since a considerable amount of over-exposure may occur without necessarily ruining the picture;* as will be understood when I say, that in the processes just before alluded to, the mode of development is *invariable,* be the exposure long or short; while in *this* it can be so modified as to suit the visible state of the picture when removed from the slide; and a strong negative may always be obtained. *Effects of wrong exposure in other processes.* *Greater latitude allowable in this.*

When the photographer has ascertained by *experiment* the time of exposure for a particular lens and diaphragm under certain conditions of light, he may then calculate *at once* the necessary time for *Rules for finding the time of exposure with different lenses.*

THE NEGATIVE PROCESS.

a *different* lens and diaphragm, at work under similar conditions, by bearing in mind the following facts :—

The time of exposure will depend on the intensity of the light in the image, and it will be *inversely* proportional to that intensity; that is to say, the *greater* the intensity the *less* the time.

Now, first, this intensity of light in the image will be exactly proportional (*cæteris paribus*) to the *size* of the diaphragm,—that is, to the *square* of its diameter. (For a circle of one inch diameter is four times as large as another of half-an-inch diameter, and so on.)

<small>The same lens with different stops.</small>

It follows, therefore, that *with the same lens* the time of exposure will vary inversely as the square of the diameter of the diaphragm employed.

<small>Example.</small>

For example, if a certain lens with a diaphragm of one inch in diameter will take a picture in one minute, then with a diaphragm of half-an-inch it would require an exposure of four minutes; or with a three-inch aperture, the view would be taken in seven seconds.

<small>Different lenses with the same-sized stop.</small>

Secondly, the intensity of light in the image will depend upon the *focal length* of the lens; and the rule is, that this intensity (*cæteris paribus*) will vary *inversely* as the *square* of the focal length.

For example: two lenses of equal aperture, and at work at the same time upon the same subject, have focal lengths respectively, of eighteen inches and six inches, the time of exposure required for the first will be nine times that for the second. Example.

For *different* lenses and diaphragms, the rule will be that—

The time of exposure will vary *directly* as the *square* of the focal length, and *inversely* as the *square* of the diameter of the diaphragm, or aperture. Different lenses and stops.

For example: two lenses — one of three inches aperture and six inches focal length, the other of half-an-inch aperture and eighteen inches focal length — are at work together; then the ratio of their times of exposure will be that of 324 to 1. So that if a picture could be taken by the first in one second, it would require five minutes and twenty-four seconds by the other,—a difference which could never have been *guessed à priori*, and which will show the importance of rules. Example.

Importance of rules.

But we may occasionally depart from *exact* rules, and adopt *approximations* to them without any

32   THE NEGATIVE PROCESS.

practical disadvantage; and the following will be found at times a very useful *guide*, although not *strictly* correct in *all* cases.

<small>Approximate rule for different lenses with same-sized stop.</small> *The time of exposure with different view lenses, having the same-sized aperture, will be proportional to the size of the picture taken by them* (or very nearly so).

<small>Example.</small> Suppose, for instance, that three lenses of the *same* aperture are at work together; that the first takes a picture twelve inches by ten inches, the second nine inches by seven inches, and the third four inches by three inches. Then the times of exposure for the first, second, and third, will be as 120 to 63 to 12,—that is, the first picture will require twice as long an exposure as the second, and ten times as long as the third.

<small>Time for a picture, 9 inches by 7, in the sun.</small> A picture, nine inches by seven inches, with a *half-inch* diaphragm, and without difficult masses of shadow, would require, in full sunshine, an average exposure of *about four* minutes; and with *an inch* diaphragm, of *about one* minute.

<small>The most favourable light for a view.</small> The most favourable circumstances of light under which a picture can be taken are, when cloud and sunshine alternate; for when sunshine prevails during *the whole* of the exposure, the contrasts are frequently too violent to be pleasing.

Figures *in motion* across the view produce little or no effect; but should one remain *still*, during any considerable part of the exposure, and then *move off*, this will certainly occasion a blemish. {Effect of moving figures.}

The picture having been exposed for the time deemed necessary *for the perfect rendering of the objects in shadow*, replace the cap on the lens, shut the slide, and pack up as before. {Expose for the shadows and not for the lights.}

FOURTH OPERATION.

To Develope the Latent Picture.

<small>A dip-candle should be used.</small>

This must be done either in a room darkened as before described for sensitizing, or in the evening by candle-light. In the latter case, the candle should be either a rushlight or a small dip, *not a composite or wax-candle;* and it should not be brought within a yard of the sensitive paper. The camera tripod may be conveniently used as a stand for the candle.

<small>To arrange the developing slab.</small>

Cover the table upon which you are about to work with one of the dark macintosh cloths, and upon the floor, close at hand, place a zinc dish, having a thin gutta-percha lining, half filled with common water.

Upon the table place the other zinc dish (which should be larger than the developing slab), and across the top of this, two bars of wood, on which to lay the glass developing slab (which should be quite clean). Then, by means of the spirit-level, level the

TO DEVELOPE THE PICTURE.

slab exactly, by putting pieces of paper, or little wedges, under the zinc dish. Any of the developing fluid which may run over the edge of the slab will then be caught in the dish beneath, and perfect cleanliness be ensured. *(Cleanliness ensured.)*

Lay a sheet of clean white blotting-paper upon the deal-board, and then remove the glass from the dark slide. When the picture is of very large size, this should be done thus:—Take out the back, and place the slide upon the floor, leaning against the leg of a table or chair, the glass outwards, then, with the right hand against the glass, incline the slide gradually towards it with the left, until the plate falls fairly out by its own weight upon the right hand. *In doing this, be careful on no account to touch the sensitive paper with the fingers.* *(To remove the glass when large.)*

Remove the paper from the glass by means of a sharp penknife passed all round beneath it, then pin it to the deal-board face upwards, and shelter it from the light, whilst making *(To remove the paper from the glass.)*

The Developing Solution.

This is gallo-nitrate of silver, much stronger than that previously used for sensitizing, *and in which the proportions to be observed between the aceto-nitrate and the gallic acid will depend upon the aspect of the picture when taken from the slide.* *(Proportions to be observed depend on the aspect of the picture.)*

THE NEGATIVE PROCESS.

<small>No trace visible.</small>
Should *no trace* whatever of the picture be visible, mix aceto-nitrate of silver and saturated solution of gallic acid in *equal* proportions.

<small>Slight indications.</small>
Should the sky and high lights of the picture be *slightly* browned, add two parts of aceto-nitrate to three parts of gallic acid.

<small>Strong indications.</small>
Should the sky and high lights be *very strongly* out, through great over-exposure, add one part of aceto-nitrate to three parts of gallic acid.

The developing mixture should be made quickly in a *clean* wine-glass (Note 14), and as nearly as possible by guess, since the *exact* proportions to a great nicety are not material. It will require a whole glass full to cover a picture twenty-four inches by twenty inches.

<small>To apply the developing solution.</small>
Apply it *rapidly* with a clean Buckle's brush (Note 14) in the usual manner, keeping a flowing edge, and not passing over the same place twice, but *bringing the solution gradually down the paper like an advancing tide. Begin with the sky.* Always use a full brush, and be careful to leave no dry spots untouched by the solution.

The whole picture should be covered in less than a minute.

Wait a minute or two, until the development

TO DEVELOPE THE PICTURE.   37

commences, and then *repeat the process in precisely the same manner with* GALLIC ACID ALONE. Use the same glass and the same brush, and apply the gallic acid *copiously*, first longitudinally, and then transversely. <small>Finish with gallic acid alone.</small>

Next,

Pour some gallic acid copiously upon the middle of the slab (which should be a little larger than the picture), and spread it all over by means of the brush just in use. Now remove the picture from the board, and with some dexterity, drain it upon the slab, and then lay it, *face downwards,* upon it. It will soon become perfectly flat. <small>Lay it on the slab.</small>

The development, which ought now to be advancing rapidly, must be carefully watched. When the dark parts of the picture begin to appear through, at the back of the paper, it will be time to lift up the corners and examine the front. *The development should not be arrested until the details in the deepest shadows are fully out.* It may be hastened by pouring hot water into the zinc dish beneath, but I do not recommend this *as a rule.* <small>When to stop the development.</small>

Be very careful *not to wet the back of the negative* with the developing solution, since the stains upon the *back* would show in printing quite as much as those upon the face. <small>Stains on the back.</small>

The development being completed (the time will vary from ten minutes to an hour), drain the paper

THE NEGATIVE PROCESS.

<small>Wash off the developing solution.</small> for an instant, and lay it, face upwards, upon the board as before; remove all the surface moisture by blotting-paper (Note 16), and then place it, face downwards, upon the water in the zinc dish,—afterwards face upwards; wash it well by agitating the dish; then change the water and wash it again.

It is now ready for the fifth operation.

FIFTH OPERATION.

To Fix the Picture.

<small>Object of the fixing process.</small> The object of the fixing process is, to remove from the paper all that remains of the developing solution, and the whole of the iodide of silver. The picture will then be no longer sensitive to light.

To effect this, make a solution of hyposulphite of soda in common water; the strength is not mate-

TO FIX THE PICTURE.

rial; about one ounce of hypo to six ounces of water will be very rapid in its action. Put enough of this to cover the paper completely into a zinc dish lined with gutta percha; then submerge the paper in this solution, and leave it there until the *whole* of the yellow iodide shall be dissolved out; which can only be ascertained with certainty by daylight. *(To dissolve out the yellow iodide.)*

Finally, wash the picture in abundance of common water, to remove all traces of the hyposulphite, which if left in would eventually destroy it; change the water at least six or eight times; leave it to soak in water for several hours, and then hang it up to dry. *(The hypo must be all removed.)*

When the hyposulphite solution (which may be used several times) gets weak and discoloured, it should be thrown away, as of no further use either for negatives or positives. *(Throw away the old hypo.)*

There is no *absolute necessity* for fixing the negatives *immediately* after their development, and whilst *en route*, although this is the *safer* plan. They may be kept for days, or even weeks, *screened from the light*, in a portfolio, without much risk, and may be fixed at a convenient opportunity, several at a time. If this plan be adopted, then all the paraphernalia of the fixing process may, in general, be left at home. In this case the unfixed negatives should *(No necessity for fixing at once.)*

be *well* washed in water, and dried in the dark, or in a feeble light, before being put away.

<small>The finished negative improved by waxing.</small> The negative is now finished, and tolerable prints might be obtained from it in its present state; but it would be greatly improved if rendered more transparent; and this is readily accomplished by saturating the substance of the paper with white wax; as will be described in the next operation.

SIXTH OPERATION.

To Wax, etc. the Finished Picture.

<small>To trim the edges.</small> First, trim the edges with a sharp knife, upon a thick board either of poplar or sycamore, having two adjacent sides accurately straight and at right angles. For this, select if possible, some prominent *vertical* line in the picture; and by the help of a carpenter's square cut the sides parallel to that, and

afterwards the top and bottom, at right angles to them.

Some judgment and taste will be necessary in determining the best proportions for the picture; for we must not by any means *invariably* retain *all* that we have got, but balance the objects properly. The shape requires taste and judgment.

To wax the pictures (when not of the largest size), procure the following apparatus:—An earthenware dish, with upright sides, sufficiently large to receive them, and which is to stand in a zinc dish, supported, at about a quarter of an inch from the bottom, by diagonal strips of zinc in the corners. The whole is to stand upon two blocks of wood about four inches thick. The waxing apparatus.

Pour boiling water into the zinc dish, up to the proper level, and keep it at a boiling heat by means of a spirit-lamp placed underneath. Put the earthenware dish into its place, and rub a cake of clean white wax (which speedily melts) all over the bottom; lay the negative, face downwards upon this, and then rub the wax all over the back of it; turn it over and do the same to the face. In this way many negatives may receive a coating of wax in a few minutes, and the heat will cause the wax to penetrate thoroughly the pores of the paper. To apply the wax.

42 THE NEGATIVE PROCESS.

Negatives should be dry.

Dry the negatives well before the fire previously to waxing them, or they will not imbibe the wax equally. Also, take care that no water finds its way into the earthenware dish with the wax.

To iron the wax out.

Finish, by ironing the negatives between sheets of blotting-paper (Note 16), with a moderately hot smoothing-iron, until no shining patches of wax remain on either side. And in doing this *be careful not to crease them*, as it would be impossible to remove these marks *entirely* by any subsequent treatment.

The blotting-paper should be renewed when it becomes saturated with wax.

They will now be very transparent, and when held up to the light may be thoroughly examined.

To wax very large pictures.

Very large pictures must be waxed differently in consequence of the difficulty of obtaining an earthenware dish of sufficient size. The best plan for these will be, to melt the wax in a jar, placed in a saucepan of boiling water, and to apply it to *both* sides of the negative with a new and clean paint-brush. Then hold the negative before a good fire, turning it repeatedly, and allowing the superfluous wax to run off by one corner into the jar again. Afterwards iron as before.

Should a negative require to be retouched in any

TO WAX THE PICTURE. 43

part, this should be done *after* waxing, with Indian ink, ground on a plate in the usual way, and to which a few drops of albumen, or a little ox-gall, have been added. To retouch a negative.

The process for negatives is now completed. They *should be very carefully preserved in a portfolio,* and when in use handled with much caution; as if tumbled, or stained with chemicals, they will be irretrievably ruined. Preserve them carefully.

N.B.—Every requisite for the practice of this art, as described by the author, and of guaranteed quality, may be obtained at the Photographic Institution, 168 New Bond Street. A price-list will be found at the end.

CAUSES OF FAILURE.

The most frequent causes of failure in the negative process are—

<small>Bad iodized paper.</small>   1. Insufficient or careless washing of the iodized papers, which will occasion innumerable small white spots, or large white blotches in the negative.

<small>Dirty tubes and glasses.</small>   2. Dirty glasses and tubes, in the washing of which the directions given in Note 14 have not been rigorously attended to, and which will occasion all sorts of dirty stains and streaks.

<small>Too strong a light.</small>   3. Too strong a light upon the sensitive papers during the processes of sensitizing or development, which will produce general discoloration.

<small>Too short an exposure.</small>   4. Too short an exposure in the camera, in consequence of which the due development of the shadows will not be attained, and the picture be defective in the half tones.

CAUSES OF FAILURE. 45

5. The employment of the same vessels for several different purposes, is an untidiness and want of method in the work, which will be *sure to* involve many a severe penalty, in the way of failures and misfortunes, *particularly when hyposulphite has been allowed to come in contact with other chemicals.* Use of the same vessel for different purposes.

Excessive cleanliness, and strict attention to directions, will in general ensure success; for the process is, I believe, AS CERTAIN, when fairly carried out, *as anything of this nature can possibly be expected to be,* and far *more* certain, than any other with which I am acquainted; and I am sufficiently familiar with them all, to be able, I hope, to form a fair estimate of their comparative merits. Cleanliness will generally ensure success.

With respect to the use of the Buckle's brush, which I have recommended for laying on the gallo-nitrate, and which may be seriously objected to by some, it must be observed, that the mode of applying the solution with this useful little article is not by any means that of *random mopping* or *daubing,* but that considerable method is to be observed in the use of it; for when properly handled, and the board gently inclined, *the solution proceeds steadily downwards in an advancing tide,* and the paper becomes wetted quite as uniformly and evenly as if a glass rod had been employed to spread it, or as if it had been gradually depressed upon the surface of a bath. And The Buckle's brush.
Random mopping or daubing not allowable.

this may be easily proved by applying a flat wash of some water colour to the paper by the three different methods, and comparing the results when dry.

Use of blotting-paper not injurious.

The use of the blotting-paper for removing the surplus sensitive solution is also considered by some as highly objectionable; but I am inclined to suspect that, if the truth could be exactly ascertained, in many failures the *real* cause would turn out to be, not the unfortunate blotting-paper (which, when clean, must be perfectly harmless,) but a far more serious evil, viz. that of placing the *sensitive* side of the paper in contact with the dirty glass of the common slide. For my own part I have never experienced any failures which I could fairly attribute to the use of *clean white* blotting-paper.

On the occurrence of failures, amateurs are but too ready to call in question the *purity of the chemicals* employed; but when these have been purchased of a respectable firm, they may be tolerably certain that the fault is rather *their own*. When every care has been taken apparently, in every stage of the manipulation, and the work, nevertheless, prove a failure, it will be well to make a fresh solution of aceto-nitrate; for should the proportions of the sensitizing solution have been *exactly* correct, the paper will either *brown all over*, through the presence of *too little* acid; or have *lost its sensitiveness*, through an *excess* of it.

Proportions of aceto-nitrate should be exact.

THE PRINTING PROCESS.

THE PRINTING PROCESS,

or that by which the *positive* photograph is obtained from the *negative*, involves the following five operations, viz. :—

1. To *salt* the paper; or, to *albumenize* and *salt* it.
2. To render it *sensitive* to light.
3. To *expose* it to the pressure-frame.
4. To *fix* and *tone* the picture.
5. To *trim* and *mount* the finished picture.

These operations are *more* troublesome than those which I have described in the Negative process; the Printing should, therefore, never be attempted *away from the resources of home.*

THE CHEMICALS

<small>For ordinary printing.</small> required in this process are,—

>Acetic Acid.
>Nitrate of Silver.
>Hyposulphite of Soda.
>Chloride of Gold.
>Common Salt, or Hydrochlorate of Ammonia.
>Distilled Water.

<small>For the violet tints.</small> Or, for the RICH DARK VIOLET TINTS, so much admired in many French photographs,—

>Hydrochlorate of Ammonia.
>Ammonia.
>Nitrate of Silver.
>Sel d'Or (Hyposulphite of Gold).
>*Pure* Hydrochloric Acid.
>Hyposulphite of Soda.
>Distilled Water.

THE PRINTING-ROOM

should be provided with a sink and tap, with <small>Sink and tap.</small> an abundant supply of water. There should also be convenient benches to carry the dishes, and the <small>Benches.</small> means of hanging up papers to dry. The window should be provided with a yellow curtain, which <small>Yellow curtain.</small> may be drawn at pleasure. A dark cupboard will <small>Cupboard.</small> also be found very useful.

The floor of this room will be infallibly stained, in spite of every precaution. Let no one deceive himself by imagining the contrary.

THE APPARATUS

will consist of—

> Several earthenware dishes, with *upright* sides, and without lips.
> A bath of plate-glass, or gutta-percha, for the nitrate solution (Note 10).
> One or more pressure-frames (Note 17).
> Wooden paper-clips (Note 11).
> Bottles, funnels, portfolios, and the usual sundries.

FIRST OPERATION.

<small>Plain papers.</small> The salting may be performed in ordinary daylight. Papers simply *salted* are called PLAIN PAPERS; when *albumenized and salted,* they are <small>Albumenized papers.</small> called ALBUMENIZED papers. These latter have a glazed or varnished appearance, and the shadows a peculiar depth and transparency. The former more nearly resemble engravings. The fashion in England just now, is in favour of *albumenized* papers.

<small>Positive paper.</small> The PAPER commonly used for positives is that manufactured in France by Messrs. Canson frères, <small>Size of sheets.</small> see Note 9. It should be cut into sheets a little larger every way than the negative.

PLAIN SALTED PAPERS.

Make the following solution:—

<pre>
Distilled water .   .   . 1 pint (20 ounces).
Common salt   .   .   . 5 drams.
</pre>

<small>See page 12.</small> Filter, if necessary; and then pour it into a clean dish a little larger than the papers to be salted. Mark the back of each in one corner, and float it in the usual way. Allow it to remain five minutes upon the bath, and then hang it up to dry.

THE PRINTING PROCESS. 53

When dry, salted papers may be preserved indefinitely in a portfolio, kept for this use, and always in *a dry place*.

When positives are intended to be coloured by the artist, they should be printed upon *plain* and not upon *albumenized* paper.

ALBUMENIZED PAPERS.

Into a *very large* basin put

    The whites of two dozen fresh eggs.
    Distilled water . . . half a pint (10 ounces).
    Common salt . . . one ounce.

Beat the whole to a *very stiff* froth with either a *silver* or a *wooden* fork (not an iron one). Cover the basin, and let it stand undisturbed for twenty-four hours. Then, filter into the dish through two layers of fine muslin, previously damped; taking care to keep the neck of the funnel beneath the surface of the liquid, in order to prevent the formation and escape of air-bubbles. Then, clear the surface from these, should there be any, and float the paper in the usual manner. Let it remain upon the bath for *ten seconds only*, and then hang it up to dry. When thoroughly dry, albumenized papers may be preserved indefinitely, in a portfolio kept for the purpose, in a *dry* place.

To avoid air-bubbles.

Should the albumen have been imperfectly beaten up, it will be very liable to form streaks upon

THE PRINTING PROCESS.

To avoid streaks. the paper when hung up to dry. In this case it will be necessary to *beat it up again,* and not to proceed with the work until the following day; as every paper would be infallibly spoiled.

Some photographers recommend to place the albumenized papers, one at a time, between two sheets of thin glazed paper, and to *iron* them with a moderately hot smoothing-iron, in order to coagulate the albumen; but this is, I think, superfluous, as the necessary coagulation is effected in the next process by the nitrate bath.

Less glaze given by a longer floatation. It is a curious fact, that by *increasing* the time of floatation upon the albumen bath, a *less* amount of glaze is imparted to the paper.

Hydrochlorate of ammonia. Hydrochlorate of ammonia has been recommended instead of salt, as being less deliquescent. It is, however, liable to contain iron; and with respect to the *tone* which it imparts to the picture, it has, so far as I have observed, no advantage whatever over salt, in *this* process.

I may make the same remark with respect to several other chlorides which have been recommended; such as those of barium, calcium, strontium, potassium, &c. I have tried several of these, but I give the preference to salt. Sea-water answers perfectly well.

SECOND OPERATION.

To Render the Papers Sensitive.

This must, of course, be done in a *yellow* light.

The Sensitive Solution

is as follows :—

    Distilled water . . . 1 pint (20 ounces).
    Nitrate of silver . . . 2½ ounces.
    Glacial acetic acid . . 4 drams.

Pour this into a bath of plate-glass, or gutta percha (with a very flat bottom), to the depth of about three-sixteenths of an inch; then float the papers upon it, face downwards, in the usual manner. Whether plain or albumenized, allow them to remain upon the bath *at least* five minutes; and then hang them up to dry.

Before floating the papers, some persons recommend to rub them with a cambric handkerchief on the *face*, in order to remove any crystals of salt which might have formed there.

Albumenized papers should be *perfectly dry* when placed upon the bath, or they are liable to become stained by it. Should this danger be apprehended, they may be dried before the fire until perfectly crisp.

The sensitive papers should be dried in a yellow light, and when dry, kept in a portfolio until required for use. They will preserve their colour and good qualities for several *days* or even *weeks;* a valuable property which is mainly due to *the addition of the acetic acid to the bath.* The acid has also the effect of *assisting* in the coagulation of the albumen, and in my opinion *it improves the tone* of the picture, particularly in the *lights,* imparting to them an agreeable *grey* tone, instead of the unpleasant *green-yellow,* which is too common in positive prints. The acetic acid, however, must not be considered as a *necessary* ingredient in this bath; since the majority of photographers do not employ it.

<small>Value of the acetic acid in preserving the colour of sensitive papers and improving the tone of the proof.</small>

There is this difference between papers rendered sensitive by the positive and the negative processes. Papers sensitized by the *latter* method turn of a pale brown tint *the instant* they are exposed to the light; and do not become darker by any subsequent amount of exposure. Sensitive *positive* papers, on the contrary, darken *gradually* on exposure to light; and attain eventually very deep and rich tints, such as are fitted to form the shadows of a picture.

<small>Difference between positive and negative papers.</small>

The nitrate-bath becomes discoloured by use. A *slight* amount of discoloration is of no importance; but in time it becomes necessary to filter it through

<small>Discoloration of the nitrate-bath.</small>

THE PRINTING PROCESS.

animal charcoal, in order to restore its transparency. To do this, put a tea-spoonful of the charcoal into a funnel of filtering paper, and filter slowly in the usual way. Filtered through charcoal.

The bath also becomes *weaker* by use; fresh nitrate of silver must, therefore, be added, when necessary.

When not in use, the solution should be kept in the dark.

THIRD OPERATION.

To Expose in the Pressure-Frame.

This may be done, either in *sunshine* or in *ordinary daylight*, and equally good results obtained. The difference is merely one of *time*. In the sun, a print may be obtained in from four to ten *minutes*, according to the strength of the negative; while in the shade, or in diffused daylight, it might require as many *hours*; but if *sufficient* time be allowed, the result will be the same in both cases. The exposure a mere question of time.

THE PRINTING PROCESS.

The apparatus in which the positive is printed is called

THE PRESSURE-FRAME.

<small>Simplest form of pressure-frame.</small>

The *most simple* form of pressure-frame (for *other* forms consult Note 17) consists of two thick plate-glasses, of the same size, with a piece of cotton velvet between them.

It is to be used thus—

Lay the velvet upon one of the glasses; on it, the sensitive positive paper, *face upwards,* and the negative to be printed, *face downwards* on that; then lay the other plate-glass (which should be clean and free from imperfections) upon the *back* of the negative.

<small>Positive paper should be dry, or the negative will be ruined.</small>

The positive paper should be *perfectly dry,* or the face of the negative in contact with it will become spotted, and *the negative ruined.* Should any doubt exist as to the perfect dryness of the positive paper, it should be held at a moderate distance from the fire *just before using.* A sort of half-light is allowable in the room in which this is done. The yellow screen before the window is unnecessary.

THE EXPOSURE

to the light is effected thus:—

Carefully convey the two plate-glasses, with the papers between them, into the open air, and place them, in a horizontal position, upon a chair or table;

THE PRINTING PROCESS.   59

the *back* of the negative, with the glass upon it, *upwards*.

The light will now pass through the *lights* (or more transparent parts) of the negative, and darken the sensitive paper beneath; thus producing the *shadows* of the positive; while the *darker* parts of the negative will, in a greater or less degree (according to their intensity), retard its action, and preserve the sensitive paper beneath from being acted on,—thus producing the *lights* and *half-tones* of the positive. How the positive is produced.

Since the lights and shadows are *reversed* in the negative, and *again* reversed in the process of printing from it, it follows that they will be ultimately *true to nature* in the positive; and the same will be true of the relative *position of the objects*, as regards right and left.

The operation of printing must not be arrested until the lightest tints of the positive shall have become one or two shades darker than they are desired to be ultimately; for these tints will be *reduced* in strength, by that amount, in the subsequent process of fixing and toning the picture. When to stop the printing.

Since the positive paper is larger than the negative in contact with it, it will present an outside border exposed directly to the action of the light. From the changes in tint which this border visibly undergoes, a tolerably correct idea may be formed of Use of the outside border.

the progress of the picture. With a *good* negative, the process should not be arrested until the outside border of the positive paper shall have assumed a bronzed or metallic appearance. The shadows of the positive will then be in the state which *precedes* this bronzing, and of *sufficient* intensity. To proceed with the printing *beyond* this point would be injurious.

The print is the test of the quality of the negative.

Should the negative be of the *proper* strength, the printing may be pushed to the *extreme limit for the lights* without *injury to the shadows;* that is, without bronzing or deepening them to such an extent as to bury and obliterate the details which they ought to possess; at the same time that the shadows will have acquired *depth sufficient* for a strong and pleasing picture, in which the necessary amount of contrast is observed.

Bad effects of too violent contrasts in the negative.
Should the negative be of *too great intensity*, (through *under*-exposure, or any other circumstance), it will be found impossible sufficiently to bring out the details and gradations of tone in the lights, without bronzing and ruining the shadows. The lights will therefore remain unmeaning chalky patches in the positive; the contrasts will be violent; and the result extremely disagreeable. Such negatives are said to be *hard* and *dry;* and deficient in *half-tones.*

THE PRINTING PROCESS. 61

Should the negative, on the contrary, be *too feeble*, that is, possessing too great a *uniformity of* tone, and too *little* force of *contrast* between the lights and the shadows; then, the positive will be *equally* deficient in contrast, for in printing it, the lights will either so rapidly acquire the necessary depth (from want of vigour in the blacks of the negative), that the shadows will not have *had time* to darken sufficiently, and a pale, worthless positive be the result; or, by pushing the printing to the necessary point for obtaining depth in the shadows, the lights will have darkened also to such an extent, as to render the picture a monotonous dark mass, devoid of high lights or relief of any kind. Such negatives ought to be of *very rare* occurrence in the process which I have been describing; they are, however, but too common in other branches of photography, and in general proceed from *over*-exposure. Bad effects of too little contrast in the negative. Feeble negatives should rarely occur in this process.

The fact that an *over*-exposed negative can be strengthened to the proper intensity, by a change in the development, is an advantage so peculiar to the process which I have described, and one of such *inestimable value*, that I may be excused for so frequently bringing the circumstance before the reader. I know of no other process in which this is possible to anything like the same extent.

FOURTH OPERATION.

To Fix and Tone the Print.

When sufficiently printed, remove it from the pressure-frame, and place it at once in

The Fixing-Bath,

which is composed of—

      Hyposulphite of soda . . . . . 6 ounces,
      Distilled water . . . . 1 quart.

Allow it to remain in this for about ten minutes, then remove it and place it in

The Toning Bath,

which is composed of—

      Hyposulphite of soda . . . . 5 ounces,
      Distilled water . . . . . . 1 quart,
      Chloride of silver . . . . . 2 drams (Note 18),
      Chloride of gold . . . . . 15 grains.

THE PRINTING PROCESS. 63

Allow it to remain in this, until it acquires the tint which may be thought most agreeable. The time will vary from half-an-hour to six hours. Then remove it and wash it *well* in common water; place it once more for five minutes in the fixing-bath; then wash it again in abundance of water, *changed several times*, and finally leave it to soak for twenty-four hours in a tub of clean water, *in order to remove all traces of hyposulphite;* then hang it up to dry. All the hyposulphite must be washed out.

The best form of vessel for containing these hypo-baths (as they are termed) is a *deep* earthenware pan. When the toning-bath becomes low, replenish it from the fixing-bath, and add more chloride of gold when necessary, the fixing-bath being *afterwards* replenished with fresh solution. The fixing-bath will always contain chloride of silver, which it has abstracted from the prints fixed in it; there will consequently be no necessity for renewing the chloride of silver in the toning-bath, as that will be sure to accumulate.

The toning-bath, when not in use, should be kept in a bottle, and the black sediment allowed to settle to the bottom. When required, decant carefully the clear part of the solution into the bath. This bath improves greatly by age. It is never too old. To avoid the sediment.

THE PRINTING PROCESS.

Changes o tone.

The changes of tone which the print undergoes in these baths are as follow:—

It should be deeply printed.

On removal from the pressure-frame the print should present the appearance of having been *much over-exposed*. It must not look *too pretty* in this stage, or, when finished, it will appear pale and faded. The tint should be a very deep brown, bordering on violet.

The red colour given by the fixing-bath.

On immersion in the fixing-bath it speedily loses its *burnt* appearance and clears up, assuming a most disagreeable and monotonous *red* colour. The hypo is now removing all the free nitrate and the chloride of silver, and rendering it no longer sensitive to light.

The deepening of the shadows and yellowing of the lights.

On immersion in the toning-bath the *shadows* soon begin to assume a deeper and more agreeable tint; and this change continues through different shades of brown and sepia, until they reach a *black*, the lights at the same time becoming of a grey, or greyish yellow. After the black, this yellow tone begins to overspread the whole picture, *and if not stopped in time would eventually ruin it*.

Use of the second immersion in the fixing-bath.

The second immersion in the fixing-bath should have no perceptible effect on the colour. In recommending it, I follow the suggestions of M. Le Gray, who thinks it a necessary precaution for ensuring the permanency of the picture.

THE PRINTING PROCESS.

A print which, through neglect, may have been much *over*-printed, can be recovered or greatly improved, by placing it, on removal from the pressure-frame, in a bath of water containing ammonia, in about the proportion of five ounces of water to two drams of ammonia. In this bath the tint will redden considerably, and the tone be in time reduced, ammonia being a solvent of the oxide of silver. It should then be well washed in water and placed in the fixing-bath as before; or the print may be placed *at first* in a strong and new bath of hyposulphite to which ammonia has been added in the above proportion, instead of into the usual fixing-bath. This will redden and reduce the tone of the print, without yellowing the lights or darkening the shadows, as would be the ultimate effect of a simple hypo-bath upon an over-exposed picture.

<small>To recover prints which have been overexposed.</small>

The theory of the action of the toning-bath is not yet sufficiently clear. Mr. Hardwicke is now busy with the subject, and has addressed some interesting letters containing the result of his researches, to the *Journal of the Photographic Society*, and which appeared in the numbers for September and December last.

<small>Theory of the toning-bath.</small>

FIFTH OPERATION.

To Trim and Mount the Picture.

The edges may be trimmed in the manner described for negatives.

To mount the picture upon card-board, employ *thick* paste* *entirely free from lumps or knots.* Lay a coat of this *very sparingly* upon the back of the print, and apply it immediately to the card-board; on it place a sheet of clean blotting-paper, and then press out all the air-bubbles, and make it lie quite flat by rubbing it with an ivory paper-cutter.

Place it under heavy pressure to dry.

The picture is now finished.

For a new method of MOUNTING POSITIVES BEHIND A GLASS, see page 72.

---

* Many photographers prefer a solution of gum-arabic.

THE FRENCH VIOLET TINTS.

The peculiar glaze of albumenized papers is by many persons thought disagreeable, and essentially *un*artistic. I am myself of this opinion, and I have spent much time in endeavouring to perfect a better printing process; for the importance of this branch of photography *cannot possibly be overrated,* since it is THE POSITIVE which we finally offer for inspection or sale; and the public, being little aware of the manifold difficulties which beset the practice of this art, are but too exacting in their demands, and difficult to satisfy.

The FRENCH VIOLET TINTS, when sufficiently neutral, and not dead, or inky, or sooty, are, I think, the most agreeable that have yet been obtained. The most favourable specimens that I have seen in this style are in the "Album Photographique" of M. Blanquard-Evrard. These prints are, in general, very rich in colour, and they possess *sufficient* depth and transparency, without any perceptible glaze, beyond that of the paper itself, when submitted to strong pressure under rollers. They resemble, therefore, most exquisite engravings, but with this advantage, that the *colour of the* LIGHTS is perfectly *charming* and *peculiar,* and totally unlike any of the tints which can be obtained by the use of old hypobaths, which seem to act by the precipitation of sulphur. The superiority of the French printing will become instantly manifest, when we place a fair specimen of it by the side *of one of our own albumenized proofs.* The latter, I admit, may be more rich and transparent, but in my opinion these qualities may be carried to such an *excess* as to constitute *vulgarity,* and that is the predicament in which I think the albumenized print will be found to be when contrasted with the other, which will possess an indescribable *artistic* and *velvet-like* appearance, (if I may use such an expression), in opposition to the strong varnish and obtrusive pretensions of its rival. Should any one doubt the justice of this criticism, I would ask him, Would he varnish a fine engraving? If not, then let us endeavour to obtain good prints *without albumen,* or at any rate without its being too *obviously* applied.

There is another advantage of the French printing (I mean that of the " Imprimerie Photographique de Lille"), that it is *absolutely permanent,* at least as far as the experience of four or five years has enabled

THE PRINTING PROCESS. 69

me to test it. I have had prints from that establishment in my possession for that period, and they have as yet lost *none* of their original beauty, although no particular pains have been bestowed upon their preservation; while in the same portfolio, works by other artists, in which old hypo. has been used as a colouring agent, are now nearly obliterated!

Such are the advantages of this French mode of printing; and the following is, I believe, the process by which it is done. I speak of course from *my own experience alone,* and from a close comparison of results; for I have never been admitted into the arcana of the process by those who practise it, and who have certainly never yet made it public.

If I am *wrong* in any part of my formula, it will be found to be, I fancy, either in the quality of paper which I recommend, or in the organic substance which I find it advisable to introduce into the salting solution. In other respects I am satisfied that the process will be found correct. Those who experiment in this direction will do well to communicate at once any obvious improvements they may make, for *there should be no secrets in photography.*

I may mention that the formula of M. Le Gray, as given in Hennah's translation, and in which he prints VERY *deeply,* and then employs *chloride* of gold before the hyposulphite bath, invariably *fails* in my hands, and is, I believe, incorrect; at the same time, this has suggested to me the modification which I now offer, and which is tolerably certain in its results.

The process is as follows:—

The salting solution is composed of—

    Hydrochlorate of ammonia . . 1 oz.
    Sugar-candy . . . . . 1 oz.
    Distilled water . . . . . 20 ozs.

Float on this, for five minutes, and then hang up to dry.

Should the solution redden litmus paper, a few drops of ammonia must be added.

The sensitive solution is composed of—

    Nitrate of silver . . . . $1\frac{1}{2}$ oz.
    Distilled water . . . . 10 ozs.

Float on this for five minutes, and then hang up to dry.

It is *possible* that the substitution of alcohol, for some portion of the water in this solution, may give greater depth of tone. I offer it as a suggestion.

The printing is to be of the *usual* strength.

THE PRINTING PROCESS.

On removal from the pressure-frame, immerse the proof in rain-water, to which a few drops of ammonia have been added; then wash it well in an abundance of water, changed several times. Afterwards place it in the colouring bath, which is composed of—

  Sel d'or (*not* chloride of gold) . 15 grains.
  Distilled water . . . . 30 ozs.
  Pure hydrochloric acid . . . 2 drams.

Allow it to remain in this until it has acquired a deep purple tint in the shadows, and an agreeable tone of grey or cream colour in the lights; this will occupy a few minutes only. The changes of tint may be observed in a sort of half-light.

Then remove it, and wash it well in an abundance of water, changed five or six times, and afterwards place it in—

The fixing-bath, which is composed of—

  Hyposulphite of soda . . . 6 ozs.
  Distilled water . . . . 1 quart.

Leave it in this until the deep purple tint shall have become slightly neutralized; about one hour will be the extreme limit.

Then wash it as usual to remove all traces of hyposulphite, and leave it to soak for twenty-four hours in water.

On removal from the water, press it between folds of blotting-paper, to remove the surface moisture, and then apply immediately, with a *brush*, albumen, diluted with an equal quantity of water. Then hang up to dry.

The albumen applied in this manner *preserves the depth of tone without imparting a glaze to the paper*. Without it, the proof, on becoming perfectly dry, would have a dead appearance, which this entirely prevents.

It is unnecessary to coagulate the albumen artificially. It coagulates spontaneously in a short time.

The proof may now be mounted in the usual manner upon cardboard, or it may be mounted *behind a glass* in the following manner:—

To Mount Positives behind a Glass.

This I find to be one of the greatest improvements that can be imagined to a positive print.

All photographers are aware of the beauty of

THE PRINTING PROCESS. 73

the prints when *in water*, as compared with their appearance when *dry*. And this is particularly observable in the case of non-albumenized prints. When mounted *behind a glass* in the following manner, they will be found equally beautiful when dry, the glass acting as a varnish, without any of the disagreeable effects of *real* varnishes.

Float the print, face downwards, upon albumen, diluted with one-fourth part of its bulk of water. (Of course I allude to a print which has not been previously albumenized, and which has been well washed and dried after fixing.)

Let it remain upon this for several minutes.

Whilst in this bath, take the sheet of plate-glass upon which it is intended to mount it (and which is to form subsequently the glass of its frame), and cover it completely with a thick coating of albumen. Level it exactly, and then apply the albumenized face of the paper to the glass.

When dry, the print will adhere firmly to the glass, and will then look as well as it did in the water.

It may then be placed in its frame.

A white, or tinted, or gilt border, may be easily

introduced behind the glass, and attached to it in the same manner as the print.

Prints coloured by the process which I have just described, and mounted in this way, are, I think, when successful, all that can reasonably be desired, in tone, transparency, detail, and, above all, in *permanency*.

NOTES.

NOTES.

1.—NITRATE OF SILVER.

CRYSTALLIZED nitrate of silver frequently contains nitric acid in considerable excess. This may be detected by the *smell*. When this is the case, it becomes advisable to *fuse* it, and expel the free acid by heat. Contains nitric acid in excess.

To do this, put the crystals, an ounce at a time, into a porcelain capsule, mounted upon a stand, and apply (cautiously at first) the heat of a spirit-lamp beneath. This will reduce them to a liquid state in about five minutes. Remove the lamp, and let the mass cool and solidify; then add a few drops of distilled water, to enable you to detach it easily and bodily from the capsule; put the lump into a glass mortar and break it into fragments; *dry* these for a minute in the capsule over the spirit-lamp, and then return them to the bottle. The nitrate will now be inodorous, and fit for use. To fuse it.

Lunar caustic is fused nitrate of silver, with impurities. It should never be used in photography. Lunar caustic.

2.—ACETIC ACID.

There are two kinds of glacial acetic acid; the simple "glacial," and the "*crystallizable* glacial." The latter is much stronger and more costly; the former answers perfectly well.

3.—THE LENS.

Use of the lens.

The use of the lens is, to produce an *image* of the objects at which it is presented upon a surface *sensitive to light*; and thus to give a photographic representation of them.

The view lens.

The paper process not being well adapted to portraiture (in which rapidity of action is necessary), we are not concerned here with the *combinations* of lenses manufactured expressly for that department, but require simply a *view lens*, that is, an achromatic lens, formed of two lenses in close contact, and in the form which is called "concavo-convex." This lens should be mounted (with the *concave* side to the view) in a brass tube, capable of sliding *easily* in an outer tube, which latter is secured to a moveable portion of the front of the camera. By means of this sliding adjustment of one tube within the other, the lens may be brought *exactly* to the proper distance from the sensitive surface, or, in other words, to perfect "focus."

Rack and pinion unnecessary.

The adjustment may be effected either by the hand, or by a rack and pinion; I prefer the former method, since the rack and pinion are liable to frequent derangement, besides being unnecessary in view lenses. Within the inner tube, and at a proper distance *in front of the lens*, should be placed a system of circular "*diaphragms*" or "*stops*," the largest of about one inch, and the smallest a quarter of an inch in diameter; and in front of these, again, there should be a cap, with which to close the end of the tube, and exclude the light altogether when necessary.

Necessity of achromatism in the lens.

In order to understand fully the necessity for *achromatism* in the lens, the reader must follow me through a brief explanation of the nature of *light*. It is then, not *light*, which produces a photographic picture (which is an erroneous term), but another property of the sunbeam termed "*actinism*," working by means of certain rays, to which the term "actinic" has been recently applied, and which differ entirely in their *effects* from the luminous rays, although possessing *some* properties in common with them. On decomposing a ray of white light, by refraction through a prism, into the seven prismatic colours, viz., red, orange, yellow, green, blue, indigo, and violet, and on applying a piece of sensitive paper to the spectrum, we find it *most* darkened in the neighbourhood of the *violet* colour, *slightly* in that of the *red*, and *scarcely at all* affected in that of the *yellow*, while the effect with other colours will vary according to their proximity to these three. Now a single lens, not achromatic, gives these seven different coloured images or pictures, at seven corresponding distances from it ; and upon focussing the objects, at which the lens is presented, upon a ground-glass screen, the *yellow* picture will be the *visible* one (the yellow being the luminous rays). So that a sensitive surface placed in the "*visual*" focus (as it is termed) would be *out of focus* for either the red or violet pictures. Hence arises the necessity for an *achromatic* arrangement of the lens ; that is to say, *for an arrangement in which the red, the yellow, and the violet pictures shall be combined into one.* By using *two* lenses of different kinds of glass in close contact, instead of a single lens, we are enabled to effect this for the *red* and *violet* pictures ; while, at the same time, the *yellow* picture will be *near enough* to this combination for all *practical* purposes. It is true that, by using *seven* lenses in contact, formed of *seven* different kinds of glass, we could combine *all the seven* pictures into one ; but such a plan is never attempted, as it would involve so many *practical* disadvantages, as to counteract any benefit, that might be derived from it, in the shape of *perfect* achromatism. *Violet rays the most actinic.* *Coincidence of the red, yellow, and violet pictures.*

A simple meniscus lens has been sometimes recommended, on the ground that the focus for violet rays, being about one-thirtieth part of the whole focal length *nearer* to the lens than the yellow or visual focus, we have only to find the visual focus, and then to push the lens inwards through the space required ; but from my own experience, I should say that I have never found this plan to answer *quite* satisfactorily ; and this, possibly, from the entire neglect which it involves of the *red* picture, and which *Meniscus lens a failure through the neglect of the red picture.*

may possibly be sufficiently actinic to disturb the focus of the other.

<small>Use of the stop.</small>

The use of the diaphragm, or stop, is to render the picture *sharper* and *better defined*, particularly near the edges; and it acts, by *reducing the size* of the pencils of light which enter, or cutting them, as it were, to a finer point, by diminishing the *base* of the cone of rays, while the *length* remains the same; but in doing this, we clearly gain in *sharpness* at the expense of *light*; still, as we are supposed to be taking *inanimate* objects, this is of but little consequence, since loss of light may be compensated by increased time of exposure.

<small>A good lens necessary.</small>

The *quality of the lens* is a matter of great importance in photography. At whatever cost, the amateur should start with a *good* instrument; and the *best* will be found to be the *cheapest* in the end.

<small>Size of the picture as compared with focal length of lens.</small>

The *size* of the picture depends, not upon the *size* of the lens, but upon its *focal length*, which may be ascertained by finding its *burning* focus in the sunshine, and then measuring the distance of this burning focus (or sun's image) from the lens. The breadth of the picture may be about two-thirds of this focal length. Or, with a *very small stop indeed*, its *diagonal* may be *equal* to the focal length. A very wide field of view will in this case be included, which is sometimes advantageous.

As some guide to the novice in these matters, I may mention that a view lens of 16 inches focus, with a stop of three-eighths of an inch in diameter, ought to take a brilliantly sharp picture, 12 inches by 10 inches, and that such a picture would include an angle at the eye of about $37°$; that is, rather more than a tenth part of the entire panorama.

4.—THE CAMERA.

This is the dark box in which the sensitive paper is exposed to the action of light, through the intervention of the lens, in order to obtain the negative picture.

NOTES.

There are many different forms of camera in use, and these should be *seen* and *explained* at the repositories where they are sold, in order to be fully understood. The most portable, and I think *the best for views*, is the single "*folding*" camera. When not of preposterous size, this may be carried by a strap, over the shoulders, like a knapsack, without much inconvenience. And even for *very large* pictures, I still give the preference to this form. Single folding camera.

Photographic views are, in general, of an oblong form, and seldom exactly square. The longer side of the oblong will be sometimes horizontal, and at other times vertical, according to the nature of the view to be taken. The camera must, therefore, be capable of taking *both* classes of picture with equal facility; or it would be but an imperfect instrument. Also, the lens should be attached to a *sliding adjustment* in the front of the camera, in order that it may be raised or depressed to suit the requirements of the view; and that, whether the instrument be on end, or in its ordinary position. To effect this in both cases, the common plan is, to mount a slide which works parallel to the *side*, upon another which works parallel to the *bottom;* but this mode is, I think, somewhat cumbrous and inelegant, and the arrangement is very likely to become fixed just at the moment when it is required to work *easily*. For myself I give the preference to a *square* removable panel in the front, on which the slide may work, and which may be placed in either of the two positions required, with equal facility; or, perhaps, better still, a *circular revolving* panel, *not* removable, and by means of which, the lens may be brought, in either position of the camera, opposite to any part of the picture which may be thought desirable. Camera should take both long and upright pictures.

Double sliding adjustment of front.

The mode of using the camera, and of focussing, had better be learnt where the apparatus is purchased; to attempt it here would involve a long and scarcely intelligible description. It will be sufficient for me to state, that the focus for *near* objects is *longer* than that for distant ones; and that in taking views, in which many different distances occur, a mean should be struck between

G

them, and the inevitable imperfections of focus, in parts, remedied by the use of a *small stop*. In such views it is as well to focus upon objects *not too remote*.

5.—THE STAND.

The camera stand should be strong, firm, and portable; and the camera should be susceptible of rotation upon it in a horizontal plane, whilst adjusting it to the boundaries of the view.

All these objects are secured by the stand in common use, called the "double tripod," which is composed of a brass triangular top, supported upon three pairs of legs, made of ash or hickory. The top has central bars; and in the middle of it is a hole to receive a thumb-screw, by which to attach the camera to the stand; and about which, when loose, it turns freely when required.

This form of stand can be taken to pieces and easily packed. For *very large* cameras, a wooden top is, perhaps, preferable. But in either case, it is well to have the top *slightly* hollowed in the middle, so that the camera may rest upon the three *extreme* points of the triangle, which ensures great steadiness; care must be taken, however, when this is the case, not to turn the thumb-screw so tightly as to split the bottom of the camera.

6.—THE FOCUSSING SCREEN.

This is a sheet of ground glass, exactly the size of the picture, and fixed in a frame. Its use is, to enable the photographer to select and examine the picture which he is about to take; in order that he may properly adjust the camera and the focus. For this purpose, it is inserted in the camera, in the same groove which is to receive the dark slide subsequently, and with its ground surface next to the lens. And it is important to ascertain, when purchasing an apparatus, that this ground side of the focussing screen, when in its place in the camera, does *really* occupy the same position with respect to the lens that the sensitive surface afterwards does ; for if it should not, all the focussing upon it will be erroneous, and the photographs deficient in sharpness. But in well-made instruments, purchased of a respectable maker, this important point will, no doubt, have been attended to.

7.—THE DARK SLIDE.

This is to contain the sensitive paper during its exposure in the camera.

Dark slides are made, either *single* or *double*. In the former, the paper is placed *behind* a sheet of plate glass ; and in the latter, two papers are placed back to back, *between* two glasses. In either case, the glass should be entirely free from all imperfections.

There are, however, in my opinion, many objections to *both* these forms of slide. The glass *in front* of the paper, and consequently between it and the lens, absorbs and reflects a considerable amount of light, and thus prolongs greatly the necessary time of exposure, while it *disturbs the true focus.* It has also the effect of rumpling the paper, as it becomes dry ; and, upon an uneven surface, it is obviously impossible to obtain a *perfect* picture. Another serious imperfection in the double slide is, that the light frequently passes through one paper, and acts upon the other, thereby spoiling *both* pictures. *Objections to the slides in common use.*

But all these disadvantages of the slides in common use, may be obviated by attaching the paper to the *front* of the glass, instead of placing it *behind* it. This is done when the paper is damp (as I have described when treating of the second operation for negatives), and in a few minutes *How to obviate them by straining the paper in front of the glass.*

the paper becomes dry, and then lies as flat as the glass. The slides for this purpose should be similar to those in use for collodion plates, with this difference, that three-eighths of an inch of space, or more, should be allowed between the glass and the front shutter; otherwise, the paper, when first put in, might touch the wood, and thus be stained; for in this state, it must be remembered, that it does not lie so flat as it does afterwards, when dry.

The back of the slide should be *removable*, and not attached to it by hinges.

Like the rest of the apparatus, this form of slide should be *seen* to be understood and appreciated. I attach great importance to it, as an *essential condition of success*.

<small>The plate-box and yellow bag.</small>
When more than two or three views are to be taken in a day, it may be managed by means of one single slide, and a plate-box, containing a dozen or more glasses, with the sensitive papers attached. To change the papers, it will be necessary to retire to some *shady* place, and then to envelope the head and arms in a large bag of yellow calico, of double or triple thickness. Under this shelter the papers may be changed, without any fear of the light affecting them.

When only two or three views are required in a day, the better plan will be to use a separate slide for each paper.

When carried, the slides should be either enclosed in a case, or wrapped up in a dark cloth, and *never needlessly exposed to the sunshine*, as, in spite of every precaution, light seems to penetrate them in a manner quite unaccountable. As a rule, no one should be allowed to touch them but the photographer himself. Let me advise him strongly, always to carry the slides and the lens himself, or to take extraordinary precautions when these are committed to the custody of others.

NOTES. 85

8.—To make the Solution called "Double Iodide."

Take a four-ounce, wide-mouthed, stoppered bottle, which keep for *this purpose exclusively*, and upon the outside of it make a scratch with a file, corresponding to the level of three ounces of fluid. Wash the bottle well, and finally rinse it with distilled water. Then fill it up to the mark with distilled water, and add forty grains of nitrate of silver. Dissolve this by putting in the stopper and shaking the bottle. I may remark here, that in weighing the chemicals, it is well to lay a piece of clean blotting-paper in each pan, balancing them exactly, and then to put the weights into one paper, and the chemicals into the other ; in this way the necessity for glass pans is avoided, for the chemicals should never touch brass or copper. How to weigh the chemicals.

The nitrate of silver being dissolved, add to the solution thirty-two grains of iodide of potassium, and shake well together as before. On the addition of the iodide, the solution will become extremely turbid and yellow. When the crystals are all dissolved, allow the precipitate to settle, which it will do in a few minutes, and then pour off very carefully as much of the fluid as is possible. This precipitate is *yellow iodide of silver*, and is quite insoluble in water. It must be washed *twice* in warm distilled water, in order to remove all the nitrate of potass and other impurities. This is done by filling the bottle with distilled water, shaking up as before, allowing to settle, and then pouring off the fluid, repeating the operation a second time.

There is now clean iodide of silver in the bottle, moistened with a little water, and this is to be dissolved in a strong solution of iodide of potassium.

To do this, add, first, one and a half ounces of distilled water, and 400 grains of iodide of potassium. Shake up well, and the whole of the yellow iodide will disappear, being dissolved in the iodide of potassium, and leaving the solution nearly colourless. Now add distilled water, a few drops at a time. Upon the addition of the water the surface of the solution will become instantly turbid, but it will clear again upon being shaken. Repeat this addition of the water until the solution will no longer clear itself again, and then add a crystal or two of iodide of potassium, in order to restore its perfect transparency. In this state an exact *balance* will have been struck between the *water* and the *iodide*, and it only remains to *filter* the solution which will then be ready for use.

As a guide to the quantity of water which ought to have been added the second time, the whole quantity of double iodide obtained should be *about* three ounces,— that is to say, it should reach the level of the scratch on the bottle, or *thereabouts*.

9.—THE PAPER.

<small>Hollingworth's paper the best for negatives.</small>

The paper which I recommend for *negatives* is that which I get made expressly for this process, and which may be procured of the publisher, at about the same price as Turner's paper, and in sheets as large as forty inches by twenty-seven inches. It is *truly excellent*, giving intense blacks, fine definition, and beautiful half-tones. It improves by age; and, in fact, it is not in *first-rate* condition until it has been made for a year or two.

I may remark, that the process, according to my mode of treatment, almost invariably fails upon Turner's and Canson's papers, giving *red* and *feeble* pictures; so much difference is there in the sizing and manufacture of paper.

<small>Canson's thin cardboard for positives.</small>

The paper commonly employed for *positives* is that manufactured in France by Messrs. Canson frères. There are two qualities, the thin and the thick; I prefer the latter when really good, but it seems to be more liable to spots than the former. There is also a *thin cardboard* by the same makers, upon which very fine definition may be obtained. Papers by other makers *may* be equally good, but I cannot recommend them from my own experience. I have heard lately of a very excellent German paper called

<small>"Papier Saxe."</small>

"Papier Saxe," which is said to be entirely free from defects. The papers manufactured by Turner and Whatman are far more *sensitive* than that by Canson frères, but they

have not the same *fineness of grain*, and consequently do English
not admit of equally fine definition. They imbibe the paper com-
solutions much more rapidly and thoroughly, and con- pared to French.
sequently require them to be of diminished strength.
The Canson paper is harder, and more difficult to impreg-
nate, particularly when thick. It is also sized differently.

10.—GLASS BATHS, ETC.

These are made by cementing, with marine glue, wide Glass-baths.
strips of *thick* plate-glass (*flat* side downwards), to a plate-
glass slab, which forms the bottom.

A slab of slate may be hollowed out into a bath very Slate-baths.
successfully; and this answers well enough for some
purposes.

Gutta-percha baths are little acted on by the chemicals, Gutta-
and are *very flat at the bottom*; which is a great desideratum percha baths.
where expensive solutions are used.

In baths of very large size, a piece of wood, an inch
thick, is cemented to the bottom; one corner being cut off
in order that a small pipe of gutta percha may be affixed
to the bath· and which may be inserted into the neck of a
bottle, when it is necessary to draw off the solution. The
tube is furnished with a plug, or lengthened stopper, which
passes through the liquid when in use.

11.—THE PAPER CLIP.

For a wood-cut of a very simple clip of my own inven-
tion, see the "Photographic Journal," for September 1854,
and some subsequent comments upon it in the two succeed-
ing numbers.

It should *be seen* to be perfectly understood; and for
this purpose I have arranged that a specimen shall be
sent, upon application to the publisher, by letter inclosing
twelve postage-stamps.

Separate sets of clips should be set apart for separate Separate sets
purposes, as when used indiscriminately the wood soon for separate purposes.
becomes stained, and communicates its stains to the
papers.

12.—GLASS TUBES.

These are to form the handles of what are called "Buckle's brushes," used in applying the sensitive and the developing solutions. For small papers they should be 3 inches long and half-an-inch in diameter. For very large papers they should be 6 inches long, and one inch in diameter. To form a Buckle's brush, force one-half of a tuft of cotton wool (chemically clean) into the tube, and allow the other half to remain out, and form a sort of mop.

13.—THE SENSITIVE SOLUTION.

I have given this of the *full strength*. There *may* be circumstances of temperature, &c., under which it might be desirable to reduce it, possibly as much as *one-half*. I have *occasionally* used it of only *one-fourth* this strength, and with perfect success.

14.—WASHING GLASSES AND TUBES.

Importance of chemically clean glasses and tubes.

I have stated that gallo-nitrate is an *exceedingly unstable* compound. It is not enough that vessels which have once contained it should be washed with simple water, for a single particle of the old solution remaining in the pores of the glass will be sufficient to establish rapid decomposition in the whole of a fresh solution, and that by a process in chemistry called "catalysis." This decomposition of the gallo-nitrate solution is particularly fatal to *paper* work.

To prevent it, wash the glasses and tubes which have been used for this compound, either with a weak solution of "cyanide of potassium," and then in abundance of water; or, better still (as the cyanide is a dangerous poison, and very unsafe to employ when there are any cuts or scratches upon the hands) in the following manner:—

First in water, then in the hyposulphite bath for a minute or two; then in water copiously, then in either soap and water or salt and water (to remove the hypo);

and finally in abundance of clean water, changed three or four times.

This washing *must positively be attended to;* or every picture in which the same tubes and glasses may have been used a second time, without it, will invariably fail.

The glass-developing slab is an exception to this rule; it will be sufficient to wash that and the zinc dishes, simply in an abundance of plain water.

15.—The Stereoscope.

Two photographs of the same view, taken from different points, a few feet apart, and on the same level, will be adapted to the stereoscope.

The distance apart of the two points of view does not seem to be a matter involving any *very great nicety*, within certain limits. Supposing the nearest object to which you wish to give stereoscopic effect to be sixty yards from the camera, this distance should not *exceed* six yards; that is, one-tenth part of the distance. At the same time, I think it would be an error to diminish this distance so considerably as some persons recommend. For *very near* objects, the proper distance of the two points of view *may* possibly be no greater than that of the two eyes. But for *views*, it seems advisable to increase *this* distance *considerably*. For we might as well expect to obtain the desired effect, from two prints of the *same* negative, viewed in the stereoscope, as from *those* differing so imperceptibly, as they necessarily would, if taken from points *very* close together. *Some* exaggeration is evidently requisite; but the amount which is allowable in any particular instance, must depend upon the taste of the artist.

<small>Distance apart of the two points of view.</small>

H

16.—BLOTTING-PAPER.

That which has been employed for absorbing the surplus *sensitive* solution, must not be used a *second time* for that purpose; but it may be employed for removing the surplus *developing* solution; and again, afterwards, if *perfectly dry*, in the ironing of the waxed negatives.

17.—THE PRESSURE-FRAME.

The *simplest* form of the apparatus, viz. that of two plate-glasses, with the papers between, is liable to this serious objection, that the *mere weight* of the upper glass upon the back of the negative is not *always* sufficient to insure *close contact* between it and the positive. I myself employ a flat board, upon which I lay a double thickness of flannel, and upon that a single plate-glass, rather larger than my largest negatives. When two or more *small* pictures are to be printed, I obtain the necessary amount of pressure by means of a bar of wood placed *across the middle* of the glass, and *screwed* to the board at each end. When only one *large* print is required, I employ a similar bar at *each end* of the plate-glass.

French form of pressure frame.
But I recommend to amateurs the French form of pressure-frame, which may be seen at all the repositories of photographic apparatus. This *opens at the back*, in order that the progress of the work may be examined from time to time. It is rather expensive, but very convenient, and many blunders will at first be avoided by the use of it.

18.—CHLORIDE OF SILVER.

To make 120 grains of chloride, dissolve 100 grains of nitrate of silver in half a pint of distilled water; then add a few drops at a time of a saturated solution of common salt in distilled water, until the white precipitate (which is chloride of silver) ceases to form. Allow this to settle, then pour off the clear liquid, and wash the precipitate twice in distilled water.

Before adding the chloride to the toning-bath, it has been recommended to darken it, by exposure to sunshine in a capsule. In order to do this effectually, it should be frequently stirred with a glass rod, that every particle may be brought in succession under the influence of the light.

19.—Ross's "Focussing Magnifier."

This is a useful little instrument, for enabling us to examine the focus accurately on the ground-glass screen. It is composed of two lenses fitted into a tube (like the eye-piece of a telescope), and it can receive an adjustment adapting it to the sight of different operators. When in use, one end of the tube is applied to the glass screen, and the eye to a small orifice at the opposite end. It magnifies immensely, and will be found very useful where great nicety of focus is required.

PHOTOGRAPHIC INSTITUTION,
168 NEW BOND STREET.

Instruction in the Collodion Process.

TERMS:	£	s.	d.
A Course of Six Lessons	5	5	0
A Single Lesson	1	1	0
A Day's Attendance ... (*and expenses*)	3	3	0

ESTIMATE (A)
For a complete Set of Photographic Apparatus.

A Mahogany Folding CAMERA for Pictures, 10 in. by 8 in. with two Slides — a *Ross's* Single Lens, No. 3 — a Focussing Cloth — an Ash Tripod-Stand.

Three Boxes of Glass Plates — a Plate-Holder — Developing Stand — Spirit Level — Deep Gutta-Percha Tray — a Yellow Curtain — Two Gutta-Percha Baths, with Dippers — a Gutta-Percha Bottle — Three Funnels — Glass Stirring Rods — a Box of Scales — a Pot of Cyanogen Soap — a Pressure Frame, 11 in. by 9 in. — Four Gutta-Percha Trays—Three quires of Albumenized Paper—Filtering and Bibulous Paper, &c.

A Leather Chemical Case, containing a supply of Chemicals sufficient for Twenty Pictures — a Chemical Chest, containing a stock supply of Collodion, and all the necessary solutions for the Printing Process — Leather Cases for CAMERA, Lens, and Dipper and Packing-Case.

All of the best manufacture ... ... £ 36 0 0

Ross's Double Lens (No. 3) for Portraits ... *additional* ... £ 16 0 0
,, ,, (No. 2A) ,, ... ,, ... 10 0 0

ESTIMATE (B)
For Smaller Set of Apparatus.

A Mahogany Folding CAMERA for Landscapes, 8½ in. by 6½, and Portraits, 5 in. by 4 in. — a *Ross's* Single Lens, No. 2 — a Focussing Cloth — and an Ash Tripod Stand.

Three Boxes of Glass Plates—a Plate-Holder—Developing Stand — Spirit Level — Deep Gutta-Percha Tray — a

ESTIMATE (B)—*continued.*

Yellow Curtain—Two Gutta-Percha Baths, with Dippers — a Gutta-Percha Bottle — Three Funnels — Glass Stirring Rods — a Box of Scales — a Pot of Cyanogen Soap — a Pressure-Frame, 9 in. by 7 in. — Four Gutta-Percha Trays — Three quires of Albumenized Paper — — Filtering and Bibulous Paper, &c.

A Leather Chemical Case, containing a supply of Chemicals sufficient for Twenty Pictures — a Chemical Chest, containing a stock supply of Collodion, and all the necessary solutions for the Printing Process — Leather Cases for CAMERA, Lens, and Dipper, and Packing-Case.

All of the best manufacture £28 0 0

Ross's Double Lens (No. 2) for Portraits ... *additional* ... £8 0 0

ESTIMATE (C)

A small but complete set of Apparatus and Chemicals for Beginners, tested and guaranteed — Mahogany Sliding CAMERA by *Ottewill*, and Single LENS by *Ross* (No. 2) for Pictures, 8 in. by 6 in. and 5 in. by 4 in. £15 15 0

Gratuitous Instruction given to Purchasers of Sets of Apparatus.

COUNTRY-HOUSES, CHURCHES, or RURAL SCENERY PHOTOGRAPHED.

A Day's Attendance ... (*and expenses*) £3 3 0
Half-a-Day's Attendance ... (*and expenses*)... ... ... 2 2 0

PORTRAITS.

Mounted in a plain Glass Frame £1 1 0
Extra copies, each 0 5 0
Tinted face and hands 2 2 0
Coloured Portraits, *in the best style* 5 5 0
Groups, or large-sized Pictures, Coloured, from 7 7 0

Miniatures and Pictures Copied, and Busts Photographed.

PHOTOGRAPHIC INSTITUTION, 168 NEW BOND STREET.

PRICES of CHEMICALS and MATERIALS
USED IN THE PROCESS DESCRIBED BY
Mr. SUTTON.

CHEMICALS.

		£	s.	d.
Nitrate of Silver	(*in 1-oz. stoppered bottles*)	0	4	6
Gallic Acid	,, ,,	0	2	0
Glacial Acetic Acid	,, ,,	0	1	0
Iodide of Potassium	,, ,,	0	3	0
Hyposulphite of Soda	(*in 1-lb packets*)	0	1	0
Prepared Wax, for Negatives	,,	0	3	0
Double Iodide of Silver	(*in 2-oz. bottles*)	0	5	6
Sel d'Or Colouring Bath	(*in 1-pint bottles*)	0	5	0
Hypo Colouring Bath	,,	0	3	0

MATERIALS.

		£	s.	d.
Hollingsworth's Negative Paper, 19 × 15 in.	*per quire*	0	3	0
Ditto, ditto, Iodized, 19 × 15 in.	*per dozen*	1	0	0
Ditto, ditto, extra size, 40 × 27 in.	*per quire*	1	0	0
Canson's Positive Paper, 17 × 22½	,,	0	4	0
Ditto, ditto, Albumenized, 17 × 22½	,,	0	10	0
Ditto, ditto, ,, 17 × 11¼	,,	0	5	0
Prepared Cotton Wool (*in half-pound packets*)		0	1	6
Glass Tubes for Buckle's Brush	*per dozen*	0	2	6
Paper Clips	,,	0	1	0
Iodizing Brush, bound with silver wire		0	1	0
White Blotting Paper	*per quire*	0	2	0

Cameras—Lenses—Tripod-Stands—Pressure-Frames—Porcelain and Gutta-Percha Baths and Dishes—Flat Glass Dishes—Scales and Weights—Developing Stands—Developing Slab, and all other requisites, supplied on the usual terms.

PHOTOGRAPHIC INSTITUTION, 168 NEW BOND STREET.

PHOTOGRAPHIC
CHEMICALS, APPARATUS, AND LENSES.

R. W. THOMAS,
CHEMIST, &c. 10 PALL MALL,

Sole Maker of the Xylo-Iodide of Silver, and Manufacturer of Pure Photographic Chemicals and Apparatus.

IN the APPARATUS DEPARTMENT of this Establishment every kind of first-class Photographic Apparatus may be seen, including:—

CAMERAS, folding and rigid, of superior construction.
Folding and other STANDS, of the best make.
GLASS BATHS, arranged for carrying the Silver Solution, thus dispensing with the use of a Bottle and Funnel.
GUTTA-PERCHA BATHS, mounted, to carry the Silver Solution for Glass Plates, up to 15 by 12 inches.
Jointed LEVELLING-STANDS and SPIRIT-LEVELS.
COLLODION PLATE-HOLDERS, for preparing large plates with facility. Pneumatic, ditto.
PLATE-CLEANERS — COLLODION GLASSES.
A Choice collection of PASSEPARTOUTES, made expressly for this house, from original patterns.
Albumenized and other PAPERS, French and English.
A great variety of Glass, Porcelain, and Gutta-Percha DISHES.
Also, a large assortment of ROSS'S Portrait and Landscape LENSES

PHOTOGRAPHY ON PAPER.

Every requisite for practising the Calotype process may also be seen in the Apparatus-room, including Buckle's Brushes, Shallow Glass Dishes for developing Negatives, with case and covers, Deep Porcelain Dishes, for Washing the Iodized Paper, &c. &c. &c.

An excellent Negative Paper, well adapted for Iodizing after the metho

Thomas's Chemicals.

followed and recommended by Mr. Sutton, price 4s. per quire, or 3l. 10s. per ream, 19 by 15.

N.B. The stock (50 reams) has now been kept two years. This paper may also be had ready iodized.

XYLO-IODIDE OF SILVER.

This important photographic preparation is exclusively used at all the photographic establishments: its superiority is universally acknowledged. Testimonials from the best photographers and principal scientific men of the day, warrant the assertion, that hitherto no preparation has been discovered which produces uniformly such perfect pictures, combined with the greatest rapidity of action.

In all cases where a quantity is required, the two solutions may be had at wholesale price in separate bottles, in which state it may be kept for years and exported to any climate. Full instructions for use.

CAUTION.—Each bottle is stamped with a red label, bearing my name and address, RICHARD W. THOMAS, Chemist, 10 Pall Mall,—to counterfeit which is felony.

Nitrate-of-Silver Bath for the above preparation may be always obtained of R. W. Thomas, ready made, at a cost little more than the price of ingredients used.

CRYSTAL VARNISH.

PREPARED FROM THE FINEST AMBER.

This valuable varnish for protecting negative pictures does not require the application of any heat to the plate. The coating will be found free from stickiness, hard, and transparent. It dries immediately.

HYPO-COLOURING BATH.

FOR RENDERING THE POSITIVES ON PAPER DARK AND RICH IN COLOUR.

CYANOGEN SOAP.

FOR REMOVING ALL KINDS OF PHOTOGRAPHIC STAINS.

The genuine is made only by the inventor, and is secured with a red label, bearing this signature and address,

RICHARD W. THOMAS, Chemist,

No. 10 PALL MALL,

Manufacturer of pure Photographic Chemicals and Apparatus.

And may be procured of all respectable Chemists, in pots, at 1s ; 2s. ; and 3s. 6d. each, through Messrs. EDWARDS, 67 St. Paul's Churchyard ; and Messrs. BARCLAY and Co. 95 Farringdon Street, Wholesale Agents.

A CATALOGUE OF
PHOTOGRAPHIC
LENSES AND APPARATUS,
MADE AND SOLD BY
ANDREW ROSS,
2 FEATHERSTONE BUILDINGS, HOLBORN.

GREAT EXHIBITION.

The Council Medal was awarded to ANDREW ROSS.—
Juror's Report, p. 274.

PHOTOGRAPHIC INSTRUMENTS.

"Mr. Ross prepares Photographic lenses for Portraiture, having the greatest intensity yet produced, by procuring the coincidence of the chemical actinic and visual rays. The spherical aberration is also very carefully corrected, both in the central and oblique pencils."

"Mr. Ross has exhibited the best Camera in the Exhibition. It is furnished with a double achromatic object lens, about 3 in. aperture. There is no stop, the field is flat, and the image very perfect up to the edge."

PHOTOGRAPHIC PORTRAIT LENSES.

The whole of these glasses give fine and correct definition, both at the centre and margin of the picture, and have their visual and chemical acting foci coincident.

	£	s.	d.
No. 1. PORTRAIT lens, consisting of two achromatic combinations, mounted in tubes, with rack-and-pinion movements, the lenses 1¾ inch diameter, and 4 inches focal length from the back glass, producing pictures on plates or paper 4 by 3 inches and under	5	0	0
Parallel mirror to the above	2	10	0
No. 2. Ditto, ditto, the lenses 2¼ inches diameter and 6 inches focal length, for pictures on plates or paper, 5 by 4 inches and under	8	0	0
Parallel mirror to the above	3	10	0

Ross's Lenses.

	£	s.	d.
No. 2a. Portrait Lens, the lenses 2½ inches diameter and 7½ inches focal length, for pictures on plates or paper, 5 by 4 inches and under. This lens produces *larger portraits* than the above	10	10	0
Parallel mirror to the above	5	0	0
No. 3. Ditto, ditto, the lenses, 3¼ inches diameter and 8 inches focal length, for pictures on plates or paper, 6½ by 4½ inches and under	16	0	0
Parallel mirror to the above	5	0	0
No. 4. Ditto, ditto, the lenses 4½ inches diameter, 12 inches focal length, for pictures on plates or paper, 8½ by 6½ inches and under	36	0	0
Parallel mirror to the above	9	0	0
No. 5. A combination for Portraiture, 3¼ inches diameter, 6½ inches focal length, producing portraits in one-half the usual time on plates or paper, 4 by 3 inches. This lens is specially useful in dull weather, or in private rooms, or when taking the Portraits of Children or Animals	30	0	0
No. 6. A lens producing pictures of a size suitable for Lockets, having the same properties as the preceding one	6	0	0
Parallel mirror to the above	2	10	0
A focussing Glass for ascertaining that the image produced by the Camera lens is formed accurately on the greyed surface of the focussing screen, and consequently on the sensitive surface of the plates or paper	0	16	0

PHOTOGRAPHIC LANDSCAPE LENSES.

	£	s.	d.
No. 1. A LANDSCAPE lens consisting of one achromatic combination mounted in tubes, with rack-and-pinion movement, the lens 2 inches diameter and 9 inches focal length, for producing pictures 6 inches by 5	4	0	0
No. 1a. Ditto, ditto, without rack-and-pinion movement	3	0	0
No 2. Ditto, ditto, 2½ inches diameter, 12 inches focal length, for pictures 8½ inches by 6½	5	10	0
No. 2. Ditto, without rack-and-pinion movement	4	10	0
No. 3. Ditto, ditto, 3 inches diameter, 15 inches focal length, for pictures 10 inches by 8	6	10	0
No. 3. Ditto, without rack-and-pinion movement	5	10	0
No. 3a. Ditto, ditto, 3½ inches diameter and 18 inches focal length, for pictures 12 inches by 10	8	0	0
No. 3. Ditto, without rack-and-pinion movement	7	0	0
No. 4. Ditto, ditto, 4 inches diameter, 20 inches focal length, for pictures 15 inches by 12. In consequence of the length of the Camera this requires an universal joint handle to rack-and-pinion movements	12	0	0
No. 4. Ditto, without rack-and-pinion movement	10	0	0

Ross's Cameras.

	£	s.	d.
No. 5. A Landscape Lens, 5 inches diameter, 25 inches focal length, for pictures 18 inches by 16, in setting without rack-and-pinion movement ...	14	0	0
No. 6. Ditto, ditto, 6 inches diameter, 30 inches focal length, for pictures 22 inches by 20 ...	22	0	0
No. 7. Ditto, ditto, 7 inches diameter, 35 inches focal length, for pictures 24 inches by 22 ...	28	0	0
No. 8. Ditto, ditto, 8 inches diameter, 40 inches focal length, for pictures 26 inches by 24 ...	32	0	0
Prisms for reverting the landscape ...	1	10	0
A Lens for stereoscopic pictures, 4½ inches focus, 1 inch diameter ...	1	8	0
Ditto, ditto, with rack-and-pinion movement ...	2	0	0
A Lens for stereoscopic pictures, 6 inches focus, 1 inch diameter ...	1	8	0
Ditto, ditto, with rack-and-pinion movement ...	2	0	0

*** Larger and smaller combinations made to order.

CAMERAS.

	£	s.	d.
A square mahogany sliding-trunk Camera, for No. 1 portrait lens, with greyed glass screen, and one plate-holder, with two inside frames for plates 4 in. by 3 in. and 3¼ in. by 2⅜ in. ...	1	14	0
A ditto, ditto, for No. 2 portrait lens, ditto, for plates 5 in. by 4 in. and 4 in. by 3 in. ...	1	18	0
A ditto, ditto, for No. 2a portrait lens, ditto, ditto ...	2	0	0
A ditto, ditto, for No. 3 portrait lens, ditto for plates 6 in. by 5 in. and 5 in. by 4 in. ...	2	10	0
A ditto, ditto, 8½ in. by 6½ in. to 5 in. by 4 in. for portraits or landscapes	6	0	0
A mahogany portable folding camera, with ground focussing screen, double slide front, with two double paper-holders, and one holder for glass plates, with two internal fitting-frames, 6 in. by 5 in., 5 in. by 4 in., and 4 in. by 3 in., suitable for No. 1 landscape lens and No 1 portrait lens, packed in leather case ...	8	10	0
A ditto, ditto, for No. 2 landscape and No. 2 portrait lens ...	9	10	0
A ditto, ditto, for No. 3 landscape and No. 3 portrait lens ...	10	10	0
A ditto, ditto, for No. 4 landscape and No. 4 portrait lens ...	17	0	0
A Camera with swinging back to be used with the *just acting* lenses, four plate-holders, and grey glass screen ...	8	0	0

Ottewill's registered folding Cameras, for sizes as above, prices the same.
*** Larger Cameras made to order.

	£	s.	d.
A superior double tripod portable stand, with brass triangle and screws, for cameras, suitable for pictures up to 10 by 8 inches ...	3	0	0
A ditto, ditto, to 15 by 12 inches ...	4	10	0
A ditto, ditto, to 18 by 16 inches ...	6	0	0
Plainer stands for the above sizes ... from 28s. to	2	10	0
Sliding Preparing Apparatus ... from	2	10	0
Mercury boxes ... from	1	4	0
Double paper-holders ... from	1	5	0
Printing Presses ... from	0	10	0
Photographic arrangement for Microscope ...	2	0	0
Glass plates, per dozen ... from			

Chemical Chests, &c. &c.
Photographic Paper by the best makers.

PHOTOGRAPHIC PICTURES

BY M. BLANQUARD-EVRARD,

Of the Imprimerie Photographique de Lille.

SOUVENIRS DE JERSEY,

FROM NEGATIVES BY THE AUTHOR.

These Prints are handsomely mounted on Cardboard, and have Engraved Titles. The size varies from 9 to 11 in. in length. They represent in general artistic studies of Marine Scenery, Boats, &c.

There are 12 different subjects, price Four Francs (3s. 4d.) each.

LES BORDS DU RHIN.

Twenty-eight different subjects, mostly 12 inches in length.

Price Five Francs (4s. 2d.) each.

L'ART CHRETIEN.

This noble Work includes Photographic reproductions of the most precious monuments of Christian art of all periods from the 8th century to the present time. It comprises Architecture, Sculpture, and Painting.

The Prints vary from 12 to 14 inches in length. They are mounted on Cardboard, with Engraved Titles in French and English. The number of subjects can scarcely yet be ascertained, as the work is still in progress.

Price of each Print Five Francs (4s. 2d.)

These subjects, and others from the same Establishment, may be seen and obtained at

THE PHOTOGRAPHIC INSTITUTION,

168 New Bond Street, London.

THE PHOTOGRAPHIC ART.

MESSRS. KNIGHT AND SONS

Respectfully inform Artists, Amateurs, and the Profession, that they are the Sole Agents for VOIGHTLANDER & SON'S Photographic Lenses for Portraits and Views. The different sizes can be seen at their Establishment, where they have every convenience for testing their powers. The Photographic Department of their Establishment comprises every useful improvement in this interesting Art. A Priced List forwarded on receipt of two Postage Stamps.

GEORGE KNIGHT AND SONS, Foster Lane, London.

SUPERIOR
PHOTOGRAPHIC APPARATUS
At the Workman's Prices.

Double and Single-bodied Folding Cameras *with all the latest improvements*, Stereoscopic Cameras, &c. &c., manufactured in the most elaborate style by MORAN and QUIN.

Gentlemen having in view the purchase or construction of an Apparatus of peculiar form, or unusual dimensions, will meet with every attention and *effect a very great saving* by applying to M. & Q.

Amateurs wishing to commence operations with the least expensive materials can be supplied with

A complete Set of Photographic Apparatus for £2 10s.

Consisting of Camera, either in Mahogany or Walnut Wood—Double Achromatic Lens, neatly mounted in Brass, with Rack-work adjustment—Portable and steady Stand—Gutta-Percha Bath and Dipper—Scales and Weights in Box—Glass Graduated Measure—Minim Glass—Porcelain Pan, &c. (capable of taking pictures 4¼ in. by 3¼ in.)

	£	s.	d.
Ditto, ditto, for Pictures 6½ × 4¾, and under	4	10	0
Ditto, ditto, „ 8¼ × 6¼ „	9	9	0

Beautiful Stereoscopic Views on Paper of the Continent and England.

AT ONE SHILLING EACH.

THE LARGEST ASSORTMENT OF STEREOSCOPES IN LONDON.

Clerkenwell Wholesale Photographic Depot and Manufactory,
56 AND 29 MYDDELTON STREET, CLERKENWELL.

PHOTOGRAPHY.

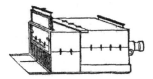

T. OTTEWILL AND CO.'S
WHOLESALE, RETAIL, AND EXPORT PHOTOGRAPHIC APPARATUS MANUFACTORY.

OTTEWILL'S
REGISTERED DOUBLE FOLDING CAMERA,
WITH RACK-WORK ADJUSTMENT,

For Portraits and Views of any focal length, is superior to every other form of CAMERA for its simplicity, utility, and portability. Warranted to stand any climate. May be had of

A. ROSS, LONDON; THE PHOTOGRAPHIC INSTITUTION, BOND STREET; and at the MANUFACTORY, where every description of

Cameras, Slides, Tripod-Stands, Pressure-Frames, Plate-Boxes, &c. &c. may be had.

OTTEWILL'S NEW GUTTA-PERCHA BATHS,
Mounted, and Warranted perfectly Water-tight.

OTTEWILL'S
IMPROVED STEREOSCOPIC CAMERAS,
FOR TWO LENSES.

OTTEWILL'S
NEW TRIANGULAR MAHOGANY TRIPOD-STANDS,
So much admired for the support of large Cameras.

The new PRICE-LIST to be had on application.

ADDRESS:
24 CHARLOTTE TERRACE, CALEDONIAN ROAD, ISLINGTON.

EDWARD GEORGE WOOD,
OPTICIAN,
And Manufacturer of Photographic Lenses, Cameras, and every description of Philosophical Apparatus,

No. 117 CHEAPSIDE, LONDON (*late of* 123 *Newgate Street*).

E. G. WOOD'S Catalogue of Photographic Apparatus, Second Edition, now ready; Free by Post on receipt of Four Postage Stamps.

ELEMENTARY SCIENTIFIC PAPERS, by E. G. Wood, Nos. 1 to 8, now ready, 1d. each.

JUST PUBLISHED.
THE PHOTOGRAPHIC PRIMER,
For the Use of Beginners in the Collodion Process.

With a facsimile of a Photograph as Frontispiece.

BY JOSEPH CUNDALL.

Price One Shilling; by post, Eighteen Pence.

PHOTOGRAPHIC INSTITUTION, 168 NEW BOND STREET.

JUST PUBLISHED, SECOND EDITION,
THE PRACTICE OF PHOTOGRAPHY.
A Manual for Students and Amateurs.

BY PHILIP H. DELAMOTTE, F.S.A.

With a Photograph of the Colossi of Aboo Simbel at the Crystal Palace.

Price 4s. 6d.; by post, 5s.

PHOTOGRAPHIC INSTITUTION, 168 NEW BOND STREET.

NEARLY READY.
A PHOTOGRAPHIC TOUR
AMONG
THE ABBEYS OF YORKSHIRE.
BY PHILIP H. DELAMOTTE AND JOSEPH CUNDALL.

With Descriptive Notices by J. R. WALBRAN, F.S.A.

With Twenty-four Photographic Pictures, atlas 4to. half-morocco, price 4l. 4s.

PHOTOGRAPHIC INSTITUTION, 168 NEW BOND STREET.

CPSIA information can be obtained
at www.ICGtesting.com
Printed in the USA
LVHW082036030621
689276LV00002B/146